Babafemi A. Badejo

Rethinking Security Initiatives in Nigeria

YINTAB BOOKS
Lagos
2020

i

Yintab Books, a division of Yintab Ltd.

Yintab Compound
TOS Benson Estate Road, Agric
Ikorodu, Lagos, Nigeria

www.yintab.com

Copyright © 2020 by Babafemi A. Badejo

ISBN 978 9789799909 Paperback

Table of Contents

Dedication

Happy Birthday!

Olumakinde Akinola Soname

Acknowledgments

I was not thinking of writing a book, at least not within such a short time. I had written three different short pieces on Amotekun and that was to have been it. When Makinde Soname called on me to say a few words at his birthday on any current issue of debate, I thought of speaking about corruption in Nigeria. Then he quipped: Why not Amotekun? He suggested the printing of the three pieces I had written as take away for guests at his birthday. The rest is history. I thank him immensely for spurring me on to put a book together on the problem of insecurity in Nigeria and possible amelioration that goes beyond the current centralized architecture.

Abraham Daniel Ameh as my Special/Research Assistant went beyond our regular interactions and assisted me in quickly pulling together this volume. He did copious research at breakneck speed thereby making it possible to have this volume that would have been impossible to put together in a short space of time.

Prof. Adeoye Akinsanya and Mr. Makinde Soname readily accepted to write a Foreword each thereby enriching the work and they have my gratitude for that.

On my request, Profs Kayode Oguntuashe and Adeoye Akinsanya agreed to review the manuscript and their critique resulted in a better piece. My Egbon, Prof. Ade Kukoyi has always been a bundle of support, including encouraging my 'can-do spirit' in putting this volume together.

I must thank my family, especially my wife for tolerating my being present but at the same time very distant as I engaged my laptop and kept the lights on. Abidemi deserves my gratitude for making the link with Rev Onuson Ezekiel of the National Library who was very kind

Preface

Nigeria started off at independence from Britain as three strong regions that resulted in a federation after several constitutional conferences aimed at protecting individual and primordial group interests. The different ethnic groups making up Nigeria coalesced into specific geographical areas. The three regions were simply referred to as: North, West and East. By 1963, the West was further divided and another region was carved out and referred to as Mid-West. Turmoil in the land as a result of political intrigues at the leadership level resulted in insecurities, especially in Western Nigeria. Police forces that existed at all levels of government even including traditional authorities were used to serve patently partisan goals. The lack of security and struggle for power resulted in a military coup d'etat on January 15, 1966 and a counter-coup d'etat by July 29, 1966. Things were no longer the same for Nigeria. A civil war and centralised command of the military after the war, resulted in the sacrifice of devolution of powers. As an illustrious Nigerian writer would put it: Things Fall Apart.

The military, working with Administrative Officials left by the departing British officials and in collaboration with some technocrats who were later joined by politicians opted for increased centralization of power and responsibilities in Nigeria. Meanwhile, corruption, widely let loose, ravaged the country.

A strong casualty of this trend was policing. In a move that was ostensibly meant to correct the ills of the past, Nigerians thought a centralized police arrangement would create a neutral and impartial agency that would provide security for all. That hope has clearly failed.

It is in the light of the failure of a centralized federation, a contradiction in terms, that there were demands from many ethnic groups for restructuring. Heightened insecurity led to the arguments in support of decentralization of policing to realize state and community policing. The federal level of governance has continued to resist these calls that started finding concrete manifestations in the last twenty years. It is within this morass and struggles to ameliorate that one must place the recent tension in Nigeria over whether the Southwest geopolitical zone of Nigeria can have what it has referred to as a complementary security outfit, so-called "operation Amotekun".

Babafemi A. Badejo, Ph.D, LL.B

Foreword I

The launching of a Security Outfit - "Operation Amotekun"- in Nigeria's Southwest geopolitical zone by the Governors of the Southwest is a welcome reaction by the Chief Security Officers of those States to stem increasing scourge of mindless killings, kidnappings, banditry, disruption and destruction of farming activities by criminal gangs who appear to be "sacred" cows, thanks to the crass inefficiency and ineffectiveness of the Federal Government's Security Architecture. While this move was applauded by major Stakeholders from various political and religious divides, the haughty statement issued by the Attorney General of the Federation on the legality or otherwise of the Security Outfit is the nadir of Mistakes, Mis-Steps, False Steps, Living in Denial, Crass Opportunism, Hypocrisy, Deception and Treachery which characterized Nigerian Administration since the so-called Annexation and Cession of Lagos in 1861[1]

It was all started in 1914 by Lord Frederick Lugard. The Nigerian colonial State Project has been described by many Observers as a mitigated disaster or an accident of history, not only because the British Raj did not conceive a State-building Project beyond the necessity of establishing control over a territory but also they understood very well Nigeria's social cleavages and exploited them in the effective exploitation of human and natural resources, the major interests in British colonial economic interest.

Specifically, not only did British colonial policies deepen and institutionalise Nigeria's social cleavages even by 1914 when Lord Lugard, much against the views of some colonial Officials, recommended the Amalgamation of Northern and Southern Nigeria

---

[1] Adeoye A. .Akinsanya and Rafiu A. Akindele, "Legitimate Trade, Annexation and Cession of Lagos and International Law," Journal of Management and Social Sciences 7 (May 2018):267-278.

Protectorates, regarded by many as the 'marriage' between the garrulous and 'poor' Husband and 'rich' Wife ('Lady of the Means'), they also politicised them in a manner that accentuated North-South antagonism which has not abated to date. Ironically, Lord Lugard who conceived the Amalgamation, regarded as a "Serious Mistake" but borne out of economic expediency, had the deepest contempt of the Nigerian peoples. In 1916 Lord Lugard noted:

> Lagos for 20 years opposed every Governor and ...fomented strife and bloodshed in the hinterland. I have spent the best part of my life in Africa, my aim has been the betterment of the natives for whom I am ready to give my life. But after some 29 years, and after nearly 12 years as Governor here, I am free to say that the people of Lagos and indeed the Westerners are the lowest, the most seditious and disloyal, the most purely prompted by self-seeking money motive of any people I have met.[2]

In a letter to one of his colleagues, Walter H Lang in 1918, Lord Lugard stereotyped the Hausa-Fulani, the "heirs to the throne," as a people who has no ideals, no ambitions save such as sensual in character. He is a fatalist, spendthrift and a gambler. He is gravely immoral and seriously diseased that he is a menace to any community to which he seeks to attach himself.[3]

On the 1914 Amalgamation, Anthony Kirk-Green has this much to say:

> The fundamental Nigerian crisis can be dated back to 1914. With greater foresight or imagination, the crisis might have been averted in 1885 or 1900, but after the decision of 1914, it became inevitable. Once the Colonial Office approved the philosophy of Lugard rather than any of his critics -Bell,

[2] Adeoye A. Akinsanya, Nigeria in the Throes of Crises (Ibadan: John Archers Publishers, 2015), p. 6.
[3] Ibid.

Temple, and Moret who proposed small units - British administrative policies inevitably resulted in the ossification of regional separation. Growth of a common consciousness could only have been achieved through lowering the barriers between ethnic groups.[4]

That was a forlorn hope. True, it is that there was the Amalgamation of Northern and Southern Nigeria Protectorates in 1914 and although the 1922 Clifford Constitution provided for the establishment of a Nigerian Legislative Council having four Elected and 7-10 nominated Members (Africans), the Council did not have Northern representation until 1946 under the much-maligned Richards Constitution. Additionally, the Council could not legislate for Northern Nigeria. While Governor John Macpherson consulted popular Nigerian public opinion on Nigeria's future culminating in the 1950 Ibadan General Conference (which actually created more problems than it solved), Nigeria's march to the cliff and descent into anarchy[5] could not be averted.

At the height of Northern Southern antagonism over many issues at the Nigerian Legislative Council, Alhaj Abubakar Tafawa Balewa, Leader of the Northern Group, and later Nigeria's First Prime Minister in August 1957 lamented:

> Since 1914, the British Government has been trying to make Nigeria into one country, but the Nigerian people themselves are historically different in their background, in their religious beliefs and customs and do not themselves [show] any signs of willingness to unite...Nigerian Unity is only a British invention.[6]

Chief Obafemi Awolowo, one of the country's "Founding Fathers" and

---

[4]Ibid.
[5]John A. A Ayoade, et.al., Nigeria: Descent Into Anarchy and Collapse? (Ibadan: John Archers Publishers, 2015).
[6]Ibid., p. 343.

by no means a push over, has noted:

> Nigeria is not a nation. It is a mere geographical expression. There are no 'Nigerians' in the same sense as there are 'English,' 'Welsh,' or 'French.' The word 'Nigerian' is merely a distinctive appellation to distinguish those who live within the boundaries of Nigeria and those who do not.[7]

At the height of the struggle for federal power in the 60s, culminating, predictably in the January 15,1966 coup d'etat, and a costly three year Civil War, Dr. Nnamdi Azikiwe, then boxed in a cage, as a result of various acts of omissions and commissions, an elucidation of which need not detain us here[8], lamented:

> It is better for us and many admirers abroad that we should disintegrate in peace and not in pieces. Should the politicians fail to heed this warning, then I will venture the prediction that the experience of the Democratic Republic of the Congo will be a child's play if ever it comes to our turn to play such a tragic role.[9]

While the race for 'Flag' independence on October 1, 1960 continued with much trepidation among the nationalists and the educated elite in the struggle for power to replace the British Raj, the United Kingdom Government foisted on Nigeria a Federal system which was at variance with the aspirations and needs of the major and minor ethnic groups, giving Northern Nigeria a **Veto** Power over decisions affecting the country[10]. Although Chief Awolowo had always supported the creation of additional Regions (COR and Middle Belt) and regional boundary adjustment to address the lopsided nature of the country's Federal

---

[7]Ibid.
[8]Akinsanya,"The Inevitability of Instability in Nigeria," in Readings in Nigerian Government and Politics, edited by Adeoye A. Akinsanya and John A. Ayoade (Ibadan :John Archers Publishers, 2015),pp.1-62.
[9]Supra Note 6.
[10]Supra Note 2, passim.

system, the Announcement by the United Kingdom Government to delay independence for two years to allow the Governments of the two Regions to settle down put the Leaders of the Action Group in an invidious situation to support Independence on October 1, 1960 with the hope of winning the December 12, 1959 Federal Election when it could force the hands of the United Kingdom Government to create additional two Regions before Independence.

Obviously, the British Plan was a cheap blackmail. The British Raj ensured "that Independent Nigeria would have to be governed at the Federal level by the North's NPC with or without the NCNC but certainly not in coalition with the AG."[11]

As events unfolded, the December 1959 Federal Election was RIGGED by the Colonial Administration with tacit approval by the United Kingdom Government and the NCNC Leadership was forced to negotiate a Coalition Government with the NPC to form the Federal Government with Sir Abubakar Tafawa Balewa retaining his position as the Prime Minister until January 15, 1966 when he was swept out of power following the Five Majors Coup.[12] To be sure, while Dr Azikiwe invited Chief Awolowo for negotiations between the AG and NCNC in Asaba following the Outcome of the December 1959 Federal Election and while the AG Delegation was holed up in Asaba for negotiations with the NCNC, the NCNC Leadership was busy holding discussions with the NPC in Kaduna, the result of which was an Announcement of an NPC/NCNC Federal Coalition Government.[13] The rest is History.

Aside from institutionalising corruption and mediocrity and destroying the fledgling Middle Class in Nigeria, one of the outcomes of military

---

[11]Ibid.
[12]Adewale Ademoyega, Why We Struck(Ibadan :Evans Brothers Nigeria Publishers, 1981);
Ven Gbukie, Nigeria's Five Majors (Onitsha: Africana Educational Publishers, 1981)
[13]Supra Note 2, passim.

adventurism in Nigerian Politics is the lopsided Federal structure which has culminated in strident calls for the restructuring of the Nigerian Federation. First, was the promulgation of Decree No 34 of 1966 which was not only preposterous and ill-advised since federalism and military culture are antipodal but also cost Major-General John HTU Aguiyi-Ironsi his life and his host, Lieutenant -Colonel Francis Adekunle Fajuyi as well as many other lives in the July 29, 1966 Sergeant's ('Revenge') Coup. Second, were a series of decisions taken by the Military Administrations of General Yakubu Gowon (1967), General Murtala Mohammed (1975), President Ibrahim Badamasi Babangida (1991) and General Sani Abacha (1997) without any serious and thoughtful consideration of the consequences of State creation (which entailed increasing substantially the powers of the Centre vis-a-vis the Federating Units) and the costs of Administration.[14] It was small wonder then that General Mohammed warned Nigerians and Nigerian politicians that the process of creating New States should not be allowed to destroy the federation as we know it today.[15]

Specifically, not only did the Military Administration bequeath to Nigerians a whopping total of thirty six States, most of which are unviable; it also foisted on Nigerians and Nigeria a fraudulent Constitution which is essentially a unitarised Federal Constitution creating feelings of relative deprivation and engendering cries and crises of marginalization and domination by various ethnic nationalities who are dagger-drawn and ready to PULL DOWN the House called Nigeria unless we embark, and urgently too, on political restructuring.[16] To the best of our knowledge and with all sense of responsibility, Nigeria is the only Federal State the World over where there is ONE Police Force.

---

[14]Akinsanya,et.al.,"That the House Called Nigeria Must Not Collapse :Restructuring the Nigerian Federation," in The Buhari Presidency 2015-2019,edited John A. A. Ayoade and Adeoye A. Akinsanya (Ibadan :John Archers Publishers, 2019), pp.177-222
[15]Gordon J. Idang,"Ethnic Minorities in Nigerian Politics, " in Readings in Nigerian Government and Politics, pp. 246-262.
[16]Supra Note 14.

The University of Chicago where I had my Graduate Studies in the 1960s had and still has its own Police Department responsible to the President of the University while the Mayor of Chicago has operational control over the use of the Chicago Police. The Federal Bureau of Investigation is the only Federal Security Agency in the U.S. in charge of inter-State crimes and Federal Crimes and responsible to the President through the Attorney General of the United States.

What we have been saying is that our problem can hardly be found in creating many Security Outfits in each of the six geopolitical zones. The launching of "Operation Amotekun", wittingly or unwittingly, is a prelude to concerted efforts and demands for restructuring the lopsided Federal structure. Indeed, Nigeria is sitting on a Time BOMB which is set to EXPLODE and soonest too. A stitch in time saves nine.

Prof. Adeoye A. Akinsanya

Foreword II

Contemporary issues are many in Nigeria. However, the security and safety of both life and property will, as human beings, always remain on the front burner. Amotekun is the latest zonal antidote devised by the South West of Nigeria as a block. But will it be both efficient and effective in the quest for security as a composite social dimension with which to evaluate governance and performance at State, local and community levels? I believe in engaging in robust debates and interrogation of depth of thought, articulation and the operationalisation of schemes and initiatives such as the Amotekun under focus and scrutiny. The socio-political, economic and legal implications should be ruminated on, scrutinized and well discerned to avoid shooting ourselves in the foot. This is why subject-matter experts have been invited to illuminate our minds on the ramifications, possibilities and realities around the initiative. Dialogue and debate are crucial social routines in all areas of human endeavors because they foster communication and understanding.

Some people have posited that perhaps the Amotekun initiative is a precursor to the much-desired full scale and wholesale socio-political and economic constitutional changes for which some people have been clamouring. Some have labelled this desire for change as restructuring. The term restructuring could mean: reset, reshape, reformat, redesign, realign and so on. But the current assertion is that the present structure is not fit for purpose and therefore, warrants a rejigging. Amotekun, being a zonal response to safety and security needs to be well thought out from ideation, to strategy, to tactics and through operationalisation in order to have the desired outcomes. Sustainability is a major challenge and continuous financing/funding schemes have to be well thought out.

Motive is the basis and very crucial precursor to the design of logic in solving problems. Multidimensional motives may result in logics that are in fact conflicting to operationalise. This results in a dilemma. When things are not right they do not endure for long.

At the federal level, resentment and disapproval are expected and more are loading. But if the view is taken that Amotekun could be structured to be complementary to the Nigerian Police Force, in terms of effective policing then that could be for the common good of the people. Comparative demographic analysis suggests that 360,000 policemen cannot effectively service 180m-200m people. We all need to be passionate in our views as stakeholders and our brothers' keepers. Both caution and tolerance are called for at all levels of governance in all the geopolitical zones. After all, because we are all Nigerians, altruism and egalitarianism should be desirable goals.

On the current imbroglio, let us agree that Nigeria's incumbent Attorney-General was misunderstood provided Operation Amotekun stands.

Olumakinde Akinola Soname

Prologue

I lived in Nairobi for 11 years working for the United Nations on peace for Somalia. It meant I went into Mogadishu where I had earlier lived for two years (before the UN's evacuation), on as needed basis. I was part of the UN's support of the unending peace dialogues and conferences.

As I am want to do in many aspects of my life and shocked by the situation in Mogadishu, I thought through, planned and concluded that if Nigeria were to implode, I would choose to live in Nairobi or Accra if I must become a refugee. I enjoyed and made friends from far and wide in the city. But I knew and know that refugees have little choices. It depends on which country and/or community is willing to accept them.

It used to be nice to take my children and visitors to the Nairobi National Park and once or twice, drove as far as Massai Mara, to view wild animals. But in all these efforts, I never saw Amotekun (Leopard).

Then came a colleague on duty posting to Nairobi towards the end of my stay in Nairobi who got me to appreciate the joy of observing animals in the wild. This became a passion for me just like I picked up watching ocean waves out of my office windows in Monrovia as I also explored the different beach points near or in the city.

I started reading about animals in the wild and followed colleagues to other parks. I had gotten pretty close to a Lion with my family and took pictures. I took a particular one that adorns the cover of my best seller book that is a dual biography: of the country and the Simba of Kenyan politics - Raila Odinga. I shudder today, when I now know that a Lion can break through the glass that I thought was protection. I had stood with my family watching Rhinos and Elephants only to now read about deaths that followed such "brave" acts. I wanted to record a close picture of majestic Amotekun in the wild but did not succeed. Of course, I knew there were some in captivity at the Nairobi park orphanage but I wanted the real thing. Not a tamed one.

Then came this Saturday early morning about 2003/2004. We had driven to Nakuru park. As we entered, my camera on my laps in steady mode, and I talked on my obsession on wanting to see a Leopard, four in quick succession passed right in front of the car. They were majestic with the cat paws design on their furs allowing them to adapt easily. Much different from the spots of the Cheetah and they don't have the flowing tears of the Cheetah either. Amotekun lacks the speed of the Cheetah also. The four Amotekun were gone before I could pick up my steadied camera. I was over-awed. We drove all over the park trying to figure out their path. No success. That was an end to one of the myths I had read about Amotekun to the effect that they are solitary. Here was a community of four.

Not until May 2009 while on an observation stop in Nairobi on my way from Johannesburg did a smart Massai guy take me right before a Leopard lounging away in what appears like sleep mode on a branch of a tree. I visited the spot twice and it was there for me to snap as many photographs with my Cannon camera. Wasn't yet the time of the ubiquitous smart phone. This Leopard that I saw in the vast Maasai Mara confirmed another characteristic of Amotekun. It is a stealth operator from dusk to dawn hunting for food, on as necessary basis and generally wondering around its territory that could be in the range of 25km or 75km radius. A very strong animal that appears lazy and shy to many, Amotekun kills its prey at close quarters through suffocation. It does not engage in the rowdy brawl of a Lion. It uses its brain to get close enough before pouncing giving the prey, another unlucky animal, no chance.

I know that Yorubas pay attention to names. And I think that the Southwest Governors made a great choice in using the majestic but a specifically angry Amotekun as the insignia for the Western Nigeria Security Network apparatus.

Nigeria may be approaching dusk. A dusk for which there may not be a dawn, if care is not taken. Returning to my thoughts, I am having the kind of fear I had some 27 years ago when MKO Abiola was robbed of the presidency of Nigeria that he won. It was that fear that made me think of where I would like to stay with my family if we were to become refugees. However, I really do not want to live anywhere other than in Eko in my peaceful home that I built with my family without our stealing a kobo from national patrimony.

Introduction

Governance in Nigeria is faced by many problems that threaten the corporate existence of the country. During its almost 60 years of existence, there has been the general problem of the country failing to have the type of visionary leadership necessary to boost national interest. In addition, the cankerworm of corruption continues to aid a downward spiral of the country. However, insecurity has of late been an additional major challenge. Corruption and leadership failure have not helped in ameliorating this challenge.

That Nigeria is politically charged and bereft of safety and security is an understatement. Terrorists are competing for who can surpass the other in wanton destruction of lives. Drums of separation are recently getting louder among many nationalities. Kidnapping once restricted to the Niger Delta has now made travels except by air, a harrowing experience all over the country. Banditry goes on as usual. Added is the spate of killings for rituals that are aimed at getting rich quick.

Early in 2018, Nigeria saw a wave of sustained attacks by some so called herdsmen in different parts of the country. The attacks by herdsmen became so intense, that some considered it a more serious issue than combatting Boko Haram. States in the middle belt, especially Benue state, and the Agatu people were faced with brazen attacks, cold blood massacres almost every day.

Factually, herders have been historically clashing with farmers all over the world. Different governments have had responses to these problems with varying capacities and outcomes. It is within this realization that one must place the inability or disinclination of the Buhari administration to address this perennial problem since it came into power in 2015.

1

Cattle herding when it comes to roaming from one end of the country to another, in Nigeria is generally associated with the Fulani as an ethnic group. Even when people from other ethnic nationalities choose to invest in cattle rearing, they tend to recruit Fulani men as labour to cater for their cattle.

In the process of finding fodder for cattle, the cattle rearing members of this ethnic group enter into conflicts with sedentary Nigerians who are farmers. What used to be cattle pathways, as a result of new settlements, and the production of other goods in Nigeria, have been occupied. The creation of a new capital in Abuja, for instance, cannot but change cattle routes. Rather than governments coming up with more modern alternative responses like cattle ranching, cattle herders go all over, seeking pastures. In so doing, they trample on the rights of others, especially farmers. Investments in crops are freely grazed upon and often times resulting in deadly conflicts. It is within this backdrop that one has to situate the heightened killings in Benue State and other places in 2016.

Though killings in Benue State and other places had been on for long, in 2016, pastoral conflicts accounted for more deaths in Nigeria than Boko Haram. Aside from Benue, there were similar attacks in Taraba, Adamawa, Cross River, Delta and Enugu States. The attacks stemmed mainly from disputes over grazing lands and farming lands. The sustained attacks left deaths in their path. Communities were razed to the ground and buildings got destroyed. There were a series of mass burials, with pictures of tombs appearing like heaps of yams all over the place. Transparency International considered the situation as "reaching a boiling point of total anarchy"[1]. Displacements from this development started to compete with those that resulted from Boko Haram.

---

[1] Sundiata Post, Killer Fulani Herdsmen: Nigeria is reaching Boiling point— Amnesty International warns Buhari, January 11, 2018

Climate change, desertification, and resistance to change as well as opening up to new ways of doing things, with regards to cattle grazing, has remained the core in the farmer/herder crisis and attacks. With lesser rainfall and increased desertification up North in the Sahel, herdsmen in their communities from different parts of West Africa are looking elsewhere southernly. Farmers in the food baskets of the nation, are keen on protecting their means of livelihood.

Chapter One

General State of Insecurity All Over Nigeria

Accclording to the Global Terrorism Index, the farmers-herders conflicts resulted in over 800 deaths by 2015[1]. The following year saw sustained cases in Agatu, Benue State and Nimbo in Enugu state.[2] In April 2018 people deemed to be Fulani gunmen allegedly killed 19 people during an attack on a Church and afterwards they burnt dozens of nearby homes.[3] In June 2018, over 200 people were killed and 50 houses were burnt in clashes between farmers and cattle herders in Plateau State.[4] In October 2018, Fulani herdsmen killed at least 19 people in Bassa. February 11, 2019, saw an attack on an Adara settlement named Ungwar Bardi by suspected Fulani gunmen, killing 11. Reprisal attack by Adara targeted settlements of the Fulani people killing at least 141 persons with 65 missing. The attacks took place in Kajuru LGA of Kaduna State.[5] The Coalition Against Kajuru killings stated on March 18, 2019 that 130 people have been killed in a series of revenge attacks since the earlier massacre announced by the Governor of Kaduna State Nasir Ahmad El-Rufai.[6]

Characteristically, the more recent attacks were usually in the forms of forceful colonization of farmlands, destruction of crops as seen in

---

[1] Muslim Fulani Herdsmen Massacres reach Southern Nigeria. Morning Star News, April 27, 2016
[2] Fresh bloodbath in Benue, 2 Catholic Priests, 17 others killed by herdsmen
[3] "Plateau attacks: more than 200 killed in herdsmen-farmers clash—Quartz Africa" see also
[4] "Communal clashes leaves 86 dead in Nigeria" 25 June 2018, www.bbc.com
[5] "How 66 people were killed in Kaduna in two days" Premium Times.
[6] Kajuru Killings: Over 130 lives wasted—Group laments.

Benue State, killing owners of farms who dare to challenge them, raping of women and young girls.

The onslaught also came with ambushes overpowering the Federal Police architecture. For example, some cases of police stations ambush were the Burukutu Divisional Police Officer, Area Commander and the Council Caretaker Chairman, who were on assessment tour of villages in Tom Anyiin and Tom-Ataan communities, Mbaya Tombu in Burukutu Local Government Area of Benue State, three years ago.[7] Another brazen display of disregard for constituted authority was in 2013, after the convoy of former Benue State Governor, Dr. Gabriel Suswam, was attacked at Tse Aekenyi in Guma LGA of Benue State.[8]

The brigandage from cattle herders subsequently moved to the Southwest of Nigeria. As many farmers in the Southwest cried about their respective losses over grazing on their investment with impunity and without protection from government, the pastoralists became more emboldened.

The situation took a frightening turn in 2015 with the kidnap of former Secretary to the Government of the Federation, Olu Falae, by herdsmen right on his farm in Akure. The news of his ordeal was of concern to many Nigerians. The President promptly ordered the Inspector General of Police (IGP) to rescue Olu Falae unhurt.[9] In spite of the involvement of the top echelon of the police hierarchy, the old man still parted with 5 million naira to regain his freedom. These criminals were arrested and now standing trial.

---

[7]Evelyn Usman and Victor Arjiromanus, Nigeria: Killer Herdsmen—That BBC Rating! Story of Sorrow, Tears and Blood Across the Country, All Africa. 20 July 2019.
[8]Ibid.
[9]Josiah Oluwole, Amotekun: Constitutional implication of South-west regional security initiative, https://www.premiumtimesng.com/news/headlines/371853-amotekun-constitutional-implication-of-south-west-regional-security-initiative.html. January 9th, 2020

After Olu Falae, many more have been kidnapped, terrorized and killed either on the highway, in the forest or even in their residences. They counted themselves lucky if they ever had the opportunity to pay ransom, and were left to return to their families alive. The victims were from every class of the social strata – from the academia, medical, businessmen and women and even the judiciary.[10]

The Ondo State Governor, Arakunrin Rotimi Akeredolu, also told his rather interesting story of his encounter with the armed men, who attempted to halt his convoy and attack him, but he managed to escape.[11]

The experience of Dr. Ezekiel Kehinde Akano, a College lecturer was illuminating. He was driving along Ibadan-Ijebu-Ode road towards a meeting at Olabisi Onabanjo University, Ogun State, Nigeria on March 6, 2019, when he was halted on the road by an AK-47 wielding male. Upon stopping, other well armed men surrounded him and he was taken into the bush. He was allowed to call his family members for ransom payment after a disorienting walk in the bush for hours. Since he once lived in the north of Nigeria, he said he could differentiate Hausa and Fulani languages and was certain his captors were Fulanis. He was told that if his family did not pay on time, he would be sold to human organ harvesters. And indeed, some people came to purchase him. From the buyer's diction he was convinced they were Yorubas. However, either it was a pressure gimmick or not, the buyers did not take interest in purchasing him for organ harvesting. He only secured his freedom after about 32 hours when his family and employer negotiated and paid a ransom of five million naira.[12]

There were several documented cases along Ibadan-Ife expressway. For instance, in May 2019, there was the reported case of an orthopaedic

---

[10]Ibid.
[11]Ibid.
[12]Author's dialogue with victim in Abuja, Nigeria, on July 11, 2019 and phone conversation on January 27, 2020.

surgeon at the Obafemi Awolowo University, Ile-Ife, Osun State, Prof. Olayinka Adegbehinde. He was kidnapped along the Ibadan-Ife expressway, on his way from Lagos. In an interview with NAN, he submitted that his captors were Fulani herdsmen and they had four guns with multiple rounds of ammunition as well as other weapons. After a ransom of five million naira, he was released.[13]

These ugly developments fast rendered the roads in the Southwest into criminal ransom traps that, at times resulted in deaths. The rampaging attacks with impunity in the Southwest got a huge press attention with the killing of the second child of Afenifere (a pan-Yoruba group that sees itself as representing the ethnic group) Chairman, Reuben Fasoranti, Mrs. Funke Olakunrin on July 12, 2019. The murder of the 58 years old lawyer, sparked a series of events that resulted in security re-awakening in the Southwest geopolitical zone, including a major security summit in December 2019.

---

[13]"I was released with N5m ransom—Abducted OAU Professor" Prof. Adegbehinde speaking in an interview with NAN, at his residence on the University campus. News report by Daily Trust, published May 8, 2019.

Chapter Two

Federal Inaction on General Insecurity

The Federal Government may have put in some effort in reacting to the state of insecurity, heightened by the killings by herders. But to many, it has not done enough to demonstrate that it is sensitive and responsive to its responsibility of maintaining peace and protecting the lives and property of Nigerians with respect to the clashes between herdsmen and farmers.

Measuring by results, not much strategically efficient measures have been taken by the government in reaction to the dynamics of conflicts, especially from 2014, as the tactics of the rampaging herdsmen advanced from attacks and at times occupation of farmlands to the use of more sophisticated weapons to invade communities and institutions.[1]

Havocs of different kinds, such as kidnapping, rape, destruction of properties and displacement of groups and killings were being perpetuated all over the country, in the Northwest, Northeast, Southeast, Southsouth, Southwest and in the Northcentral. In most cases, the official response from the government has been mere condemnations of such, without concrete actions, or seeing that justice is served to the letter.

---

[1]Jude Okwudili Odigbo, "Grazing Conundrum: Herdsmen-Farmers Conflict and Internal Security Crisis" in Oshita O. Oshita et. al., (eds), Internal Security Management in Nigeria (London: Palgrave Macmillan, 2019), pp 99-121.

It is important to state that destructive incursions of Fulani herders into the Southwest of Nigeria predates the presidency of Muhammadu Buhari. It has been very historical. However, in a more recent history, and precisely about two decades ago, in a herder/farmer clash at Oke-Ogun, in Oyo State, the shoe was on the wrong foot and cattle owner Muhammadu Buhari reacted swiftly. On October 13, 2000, Major-General Muhammadu Buhari, a private citizen led a high-powered delegation that included Major-General Buba Marwa, a former governor of Lagos State; Alhaji Aliko Muhammed; Alhaji Abdulrazak and Alhaji Hassan to Oyo-State that was then under the governorship of late Alhaji Lam Adeshina.[2] Major-General Buhari alleged that sixty-eight Fulani herders had been killed at Oke-Ogun. According to Agbaakin Kehinde Olaosebikan, then Chief Press Secretary to the Governor, citizen Buhari was emitting fire as he accused the Governor of complicity in the alleged murders.[3] In Major-General Buhari's words:

> Your Excellency, our visit here is to discuss with you and your government our displeasure about the incident of clashes between two peoples… the Fulani cattle rearers and merchants are today being harassed, attacked and killed like in Saki. In the month of May 2000, 68 bodies of Fulani cattle rearers were recovered and buried under the supervision and protection from a team of Mobile Police from Oyo State Command". That some arrests were made by Oyo State Police Command in the massacre with their immediate release without court trial. This was said to have been ordered by Oyo State authorities and they were so released to their amazement. The release of the arrested suspects gave the clear impression that the authorities are backing and protecting them to continue the unjust and illegal killings of Fulani cattle rearers…[4]

---

[2]https://www.independent.ng/herdsmen-farmers-clash-eyes-buhari/
[3]Ibid.
[4]Temidayo Akinsuyi, "Herdsmen/Farmers Clash: All Eyes On Buhari", January 9, 2018 in https://www.independent.ng/herdsmen-farmers-clash-eyes-buhari/

With a militarized mien, cattle owner Buhari demanded that the killings must stop, justice must be meted out and compensation paid.

The Governor asked the Commissioner of Police and the Director of State Security Service – both federal government appointees, who were present at the meeting to speak. The first to speak was the Commissioner of Police who stated that:

"The killing of the natives by the Fulanis was duly reported to the police and, of course, we can't make arrest because, as soon as they kill, they migrate to other areas. Who are you going to arrest? That is the problem".[5]

The killing of some Fulani herders was a result of "piled up anger", the Commissioner disclosed that arrests had been made and the suspects were in police custody. The Director of State Security Services in his intervention stated that:

> The natives don't have problem with the Fulanis who are resident but those who are coming in, they don't care about anybody. They just go ahead and when they graze the natives farms, whoever cares to challenge them runs into trouble. You said 68 people were killed and people driven away. I am not saying there were no killings but they cannot be more than five. The petition is on the harsh side, there is nothing like that.[6]

The Governor did not have to say much. He among other things noted:

> I want to say also that we really have to appeal to our people, the itinerant Bororo people, that they should observe less aggression. It is not good, it is not right just coming from somewhere then you just pass through farm lands cultivated

---

[5]Ibid.
[6]Ibid.

10

may be with the person's life savings and then over night everything is gone. That is not right, even Allah does not approve of that…We even wonder when they talk about this people carrying dangerous weapons, I say do they really believe in Allah? When you just take life like that and go away! Are we not forbidden not to take human life? So I think General Buhari, General Marwa, you have to be educating them… It is my pleasure to inform you that at the Presidential Lodge, we have made some arrangements for refreshments so that before you go we can refresh together.[7]

A disgruntled delegation of cattle owners uncivilly refused to partake of the refreshments that had been provided.

With Muhammadu Buhari, now as President of Nigeria, much was expected. But his body language in office appears insensitive. President Muhammadu Buhari as well as a number of political and traditional leaders, including the Emir of Kano, in northern Nigeria are reported to be life patrons of the Miyetti Allah Cattle Breeders Association of Nigeria. These leaders have not denied such claims.

The least a national leader could have done would be for the President to temporarily, while in office, withdraw his relationship with any cattle herders association. Even without instructions, such simple action would be a message to law enforcement agencies that they can carry out their tasks without fears of reproach from sycophants in the presidency.

Initially, the President did not play his good offices role as father of the nation by paying visits to places where pastoralists-farmers clashes had cost lives. A good example was the killing of 73 people in Benue state on January 1, 2018. The President only undertook a generalist visit to the

---

[7]Ibid.

state well over three months later. There was also the massacre in the Plateau state in June 2018. The President only reacted to condemnation of his sending the Vice-President to Plateau state to commiserate with the government and people on the killing of 100 persons. He followed a day after the visit of the Vice-President.[8]

The Executive sought to solve the problems by seeking to set up cattle colonies in the different states of the federation. The varying statements continued to be refined under different names with the most recent being rural grazing areas (RUGA). Ruga or rugga, as a word, as opposed to the acronym has its etymology in the Fulani language. It reportedly means human settlement.[9] The concept inflamed people who saw a federal design to take over their ancestral lands for the settlement of the President's ethnic group. Initially, there was no clarification that all Nigerians would be supported to enter into the business of cattle ranching as was the case immediately before, and much so after independence when Chief Obafemi Awolowo set up ranches in many parts of what was then known as Western Region where he was the Premier.

Flippantly, the presidential Special Adviser on Media and Publicity, Femi Adesina did not help matters when he went on television and asked people to be happy to have the option of surrendering their ancestral land instead of being killed for it.[10] This insensitive statement was interpreted as the federal government endorsing forceful takeover of land as well as open grazing by the President's ethnic group.

Garba Shehu, the President's Senior Special Assistant on Media and Publicity in a statement in Abuja sought to allay fears when he explained that beneficiaries of the Ruga Settlement would include all persons in

---

[8]Samson Toromade, Pulse News, June 27, 2018.
[9]Please see, ibid
[10]Special Adviser to the President on Media and Publicity, Chief Femi Adesina, speaking on AIT morning programme. Emmanuel Aziken and Dennis Agbo, writing for Vanguard News, captured the story as "Giving Land for ranching better than death—Presidency" July 4, 2018

livestock business and not only Fulani herders. The settlements as allure to stop open grazing that was breeding conflict between farmers and herders as well as improve the value chain on production of animal proteins, would have such amenities, including schools, hospitals, road networks, veterinary clinics, markets and manufacturing entities that would process and add value to meats and animal products.

However, the feeble efforts of the President in asking Ibrahim Idris, the then Inspector General of Police to proceed to Benue (which the latter ignored and without any sanction), did not reduce insecurities all over Nigeria, including in the Southwest geopolitical zone.

On the contrary and in spite of the claims and cries of victims on being confronted by herders with AK-47, President Buhari constantly repeated that herders in Nigeria only carry sticks and machetes for self-defense. This was his message to Justin Welby, the Archbishop of Canterbury and President Donald Trump.[11] Of course, it is possible that criminals seeing that Fulanis were enjoying relative immunities from security forces may be mimicking the Fulani as a way to escape from being brought to book.

Meanwhile, Yakubu Dogara, then Speaker of the House of Representatives, July 2, 2018 stated that history will be harsh on the Buhari administration if it fails to stop the mass killing of innocent Nigerians. He argued that the unresolved rampant killings of defenseless people, including innocent and vulnerable children and women, in various parts of the country, called for sober reflection. He called for more concerted efforts by the National Assembly to exploit all its constitutional powers and privileges to ensure the protection of lives and property in the country under the auspices of security agencies.[12]

---

[11]See, ibid.
[12]Speaker of the House of Representatives, Mr. Yakubu Dogara stated this while welcoming members back from the Eid-El-Fitr holiday. Emmanuel Aziken and Dennis Agbo, writing for Vanguard News, captured the story as "Giving Land for ranching better than death—Presidency" July 4, 2018

Chapter Three

Reactions to the Federal Government's Inaction

The lethargy with which the Federal government of Nigeria handled the crisis enveloping much of the country with respect to herders-farmers clashes and criminality being presented as operations by Fulani militants wreaking havoc in the nation did not please many Nigerians. Varying reactions to the woes came from Civil Society Organisations (CSOs), religious organisations as well as non-partisan national leaders.

The Executive Director, Rule of Law and Accountability Advocacy Centre, RULAAC, Okechukwu Nwanguma, was one of those who added his voice to many CSO leaders who commented on the rampaging in the nation by suspected herdsmen. He stated: "herdsmen have been linked to hundreds of killings and mass atrocities across the country. They have been linked to cases of invasion of communities, rape and rated the third deadliest terrorist group in the world. Government has not demonstrated that it is concerned about the high number of human lives and property destroyed by this bloodthirsty murderers and criminals. It has failed in its primary duty of guaranteeing security"[1]

Speaking in a similar vein, the Christian Association of Nigeria, CAN, through its Secretary, Dr. Joseph Ajujungwa expressed concerns that

---

[1] Evelyn Usman and Victor Arjiromanus, Nigeria: Killer Herdsmen—That BBC Rating! Story of Sorrow, Tears and Blood Across the Country, All Africa. 20 July 2019.

insecurity could threaten the 2019 polls.[2] CAN did not only bemoan the menace of herders and criminal attacks but also said it was a sign of total collapse of the security architecture in Nigeria. CAN spoke as reactions, at the time, trailed the killing of over 100 residents of Plateau State by suspected herdsmen. Making the point about the impotence of governments to address insecurity, Dr. Ajujungwa stated:

> CAN is saddened that many days after that avoidable massacre of innocent Nigerians in Plateau State, government is still telling the same old-fashioned stories. "For every murderous act of these marauders, the Federal Government and the security agencies reel out words of assurance that never yield any fruit. "We restate once again that the incessant, senseless and wicked killings going on in the Middle Belt and South-East is totally unacceptable to us."[3]

Ajujungwa said it was more lamentable that whereas government had never prosecuted any of the AK-47 wielding-herdsmen, who had murdered hundreds of Nigerians, it rushed to convict to death, five Christians for allegedly killing one of the attackers. "There is grave injustice in this country and they are not even pretending about it. These people are using AK 47, killing everybody; almost 200 were killed in Jos but the police never arrested any, army never arrested any, and we are saying there is security? There is no security in Nigeria, "We are calling on the Federal Government; if we have security, let them rise to the challenge. This is not good for this democracy, especially at a time we are preparing for election and such thing is happening, I don't think it is in the best interest of Nigeria. It is putting the election in jeopardy.

On Tuesday, 16th July, 2019, things took a different turn in Abuja, with the Northern Elders Forum (NEF) and the Coalition of the Northern

---

[2]See, Vanguard News, in the story, "Giving land for ranching better than death – Presidency" July 4, 2018
[3]Ibid

Groups CNGs ordering Fulani herdsmen to leave the Southern parts of the country and return to the North where their safety and those of their cows would be guaranteed. NEF's Chairman, Prof Ango Abdullahi, at a conference, said the call became necessary upon realization that the lives of Fulani herders were put at risk due to actions and utterances of some Southern leaders, especially since the death of Fasoranti's daughter, alleging that some leaders in the south were using the incident to instigate all forms of violence against the northerners.[4]

That Nigeria was politically charged and bereft of safety and security would be an understatement. Terrorists were competing for who can surpass the other in wanton destruction of lives. Drums of separation were getting louder among many nationalities.[5] The situation, rather than improve, continued to worsen.

Former President Olusegun Obasanjo, remains very much actively involved in the affairs of Nigeria, his country. For instance, as an elder statesman, even before President Buhari, he paid a condolence visit to Benue state over the massacre of 73 persons on New Year's day in 2018.[6]

He listened to the pains of the people of Benue State through the Governor and other elected leaders before visiting the 73 graves to lay a wreath. Privately and publicly, he constantly held meetings with several stakeholders with the aim of reducing tension and find solutions to the problem of insecurity in Nigeria.

Former President Olusegun Obasanjo chose the opportunity of the delivery of a keynote address at the Cathedral Church of St. Paul's

---

[4] For details, see AllAfrica, July 20, 2019
[5] Babafemi Badejo, writing on his takeaways from deliberations at the Abdulsalami Abubakar Institute for Peace and Sustainable Development Studies. See The Nation, Instability in Nigeria: The Maizube Farm deliberations, 6th August, 2019
[6] https://punchng.com/obasanjo-in-benue-visits-gravesite-of-73-herdsmen-victims/

Anglican Church, in Oleh, the administrative capital of Isoko South Local Government Area of Delta State on May 18, 2019 to warn against what he described as a plot to Fulanise West Africa and Islamise Africa.[7]

His statement became very controversial. While he received knocks from some people from Northern Nigeria, He had the full support of the Christian Elders Forum.[8] Equally, Prof. Wole Soyinka put his long time differences with Obasanjo aside and urged the government to take a closer look at Obasanjo's Fulanisation statement and find ways to ameliorate the insecurities in the country.[9] Former Governor Sule Lamido, on the contrary, chastised Obasanjo over the Fulanisation and Islamisation statement.[10]

Nonetheless, the former President was not deterred. On July 15, 2019, former President Obasanjo issued an open letter to President Buhari. This letter is reproduced below in full:

Open Letter to President, General Muhammadu Buhari

I am constrained to write to you this open letter. I decided to make it an open letter because the issue is very weighty and must be greatly worrisome to all concerned Nigerians and that means all right-thinking Nigerians and those resident in Nigeria.

Since the issue is of momentous concern to all well-meaning and all right-thinking Nigerians, it must be of great concern to you, and collective thinking and dialoguing is the best way of finding an appropriate and adequate solution to the problem.

---

[7] Matthew Omonigho, Obasanjo speaks on insecurity in Nigeria, reveals who government must contact. May 18, 2019
[8] Fulanisation: We're hundred percent behind Obasanjo – Christian Elders ON MAY 24, 2019. Read more at: https://www.vanguardngr.com/2019/05/fulanisation-were-hundred-percent-behind-obasanjo-christian-elders/
[9] https://www.thecable.ng/soyinka-to-fg-dont-ignore-obasanjos-comment-on-insecurity
[10] https://www.independent.ng/boko-haram-dont-be-a-bigot-sule-lamido-lambasts-obasanjo/

The contents of this letter, therefore, should be available to all those who can help in proffering effective solutions for the problem of insecurity in the land. One of the spinoffs and accelerants is the misinformation and disinformation through the use of fake news. A number of articles, in recent days, have been attributed to me by some people who I believe may be seeking added credence and an attentive audience for their opinions and view-points. As you know very well, I will always boldly own what I say and disown what is put into my mouth

But the issue I am addressing here is very serious; it is the issue of life and death for all of us and for our dear country, Nigeria. This issue can no longer be ignored, treated with nonchalance, swept under the carpet or treated with cuddling glove. The issue is hitting at the foundation of our existence as Nigerians and fast eroding the root of our Nigerian community.

I am very much worried and afraid that we are on the precipice and dangerously reaching a tipping point where it may no longer be possible to hold danger at bay.

Without being immodest, as a Nigerian who still bears the scar of the Nigerian civil war on my body and with a son who bears the scar of fighting Boko Haram on his body, you can understand, I hope, why I am so concerned.

When people are desperate and feel that they cannot have confidence in the ability of government to provide security for their lives and properties, they will take recourse to anything and everything that can guarantee their security individually and collectively.

For over ten years, for four of which you have been the captain of the ship, Boko Haram has menacingly ravaged the land and in spite of government's claim of victory over Boko Haram, the

18

potency and the activities of Boko Haram, where they are active, remain undiminished, putting lie to government's claim. The recent explanation of the Chief of Army Staff for non-victory due to lack of commitment and lack of motivation on the part of troops bordering on sabotage speaks for itself.

Say what you will, Boko Haram is still a daily issue of insecurity for those who are victimised, killed, maimed, kidnapped, raped, sold into slavery and forced into marriage and for children forcibly recruited into carrying bombs on them to detonate among crowds of people to cause maximum destructions and damage. And Boko Haram will not go away on the basis of sticks alone, carrots must overweigh sticks. How else do you deal with issues such as only about 50% literacy in North-East with over 70% unemployment?

Herdsmen/farmers crises and menace started with government treating the issue with cuddling glove instead of hammer. It has festered and spread. Today, it has developed into banditry, kidnapping, armed robbery and killings all over the country.

The unfortunate situation is that the criminality is being perceived as a 'Fulani' menace unleashed by Fulani elite in the different parts of the country for a number of reasons but even more unfortunately, many Nigerians and non-Nigerians who are friends of Nigeria attach vicarious responsibility to you as a Fulani elite and the current captain of the Nigeria ship. Perception may be as potent as reality at times.

Whatever may be the grievances of Fulanis, if any, they need to be put out in the open and their grievances, if legitimate, be addressed; and if other ethnic groups have grievances, let them also be brought out in the open and addressed through debate and dialogue.

The main issue, if I may dare say, is poor management or mismanagement of diversity which, on the other hand, is one of our greatest and most important assets. As a result, very onerous cloud is gathering. And rain of destruction, violence, disaster and disunity can only be the outcome.

Nothing should be taken for granted, the clock is ticking with the cacophony of dissatisfaction and disaffection everywhere in and outside the country. The Presidency and the Congress in the US have signalled to us to put our house in order. The House of Lords in the UK had debated the Nigerian security situation. We must understand and appreciate the significance, implication and likely consequences of such concerns and deliberations.

No one can stop hate speech, violent agitation and smouldering violent agitation if he fans the embers of hatred, disaffection and violence. It will continue to snowball until it is out of control. A stich in time saves nine, goes the old wise saying.

With the death of Funke, Chief Fasoranti's daughter, some sympathetic Nigerian groups are saying "enough is enough". Prof. Anya, a distinguished Nigerian merit Laureate, has this to say "We can no longer say with certainty that we have a nation". Niger-Delta leaders, South-Eastern leaders, Middle-Belt leaders and Northern Elders Forum have not remained quiet. Different ordinary Nigerians at home and abroad are calling for different measures to address or ameliorate the situation.
All the calls and cries can only continue to be ignored at the expense of Nigerian unity, if not its continued existence. To be explicit and without equivocation, Mr. President and General, I am deeply worried about four avoidable calamities:

(i)   abandoning Nigeria into the hands of criminals who are all being suspected, rightly or wrongly, as Fulanis and

20

terrorists of Boko Haram type;

(ii)   spontaneous or planned reprisal attacks against Fulanis which may inadvertently or advertently mushroom into pogrom or Rwanda-type genocide that we did not believe could happen and yet it happened.

(iii)   similar attacks against any other tribe or ethnic group anywhere in the country initiated by rumours, fears, intimidation and revenge capable of leading to pogrom;

(iv)   violent uprising beginning from one section of the country and spreading quickly to other areas and leading to dismemberment of the country.

It happened to Yugoslavia not too long ago. If we do not act now, one or all of these scenarios may happen. We must pray and take effective actions at the same time.

The initiative is in the hands of the President of the nation, but he cannot do it alone. In my part of the world, if you are sharpening your cutlass and a mad man comes from behind to take the cutlass from you, you need other people's assistance to have your cutlass back without being harmed.

The mad men with serious criminal intent and terrorism as core value have taken cutlass of security. The need for assistance to regain control is obviously compelling and must be embraced now.

A couple of weeks ago at a public lecture, I had said, among other things, that:

"In all these issues of mobilisation for national unity, stability, security, cooperation, development, growth and progress, there is no consensus.

"Like in the issue of security, government should open up

21

discussion, debate and dialogue as part of consultation at different levels and the outcome of such deliberations should be collated to form inputs into a national conference to come up with the solution that will effectively deal with the issues and lead to rapid development, growth and progress which will give us a wholesome society and enhanced living standard and livelihood in an inclusive and shared society.

"It will be a national programme. We need unity of purpose and nationally accepted strategic roadmap that will not change with whims and caprices of any government. It must be owned by the citizens, people's policy and strategy implemented by the government no matter its colour and leaning.

"Some of the groups that I will suggest to be contacted are: traditional rulers, past heads of service (no matter how competent or incompetent they have been and how much they have contributed to the mess we are in), past heads of para-military organisations, private sector, civil society, community leaders particularly in the most affected areas, present and past governors, present and past local government leaders, religious leaders, past Heads of State, past intelligence chiefs, past Heads of Civil Service and relevant current and retired diplomats, members of opposition and any groups that may be deemed relevant."

The President must be seen to be addressing this issue with utmost seriousness and with maximum dispatch and getting all hands on deck to help. If there is failure, the principal responsibility will be that of the President and no one else.

We need cohesion and concentration of effort and maximum force – political, economic, social, psychological and military – to deal successfully with the menace of criminality and terrorism separately and together. Blame game among own

22

forces must be avoided. It is debilitating and only helpful to our adversary.

We cannot dither anymore. It is time to confront this threat headlong and in a manner that is holistic, inclusive and purposeful. For the sake of Nigeria and Nigerians, I pray that God may grant you, as our President, the wisdom, the understanding, the political will and the courage to do what is right when it is right and without fear or favour.

May God save, secure, protect and bless Nigeria. May He open to us a window of opportunity that we can still use to prevent the worst happening. As we say in my village, "May God forbid bad thing".

Olusegun Obasanjo
July 15, 2019

Former President Obasanjo did not receive any open reply. The President of Nigeria was mum.

With tension unabated in the country, former Head of State, General Abdulsalami Abubakar, used the platform of the Abdulsalami Abubakar Institute for Peace and Sustainable Development Studies to invite 70 Nigerians to Maizube Farms, Minna, Niger State, Nigeria, for a Roundtable on National and Security Issues for Political Stability from 29th - 30th July, 2019. In short, the Roundtable was to deliberate on the way out of the insecurity in Nigeria.

Claimants to the representations of major nationalities in the North Central, South-West, South-East and South-South fired a salvo on the eve of the Roundtable. They indicated they had unraveled an attempt to suck them into a meeting with a trade association that has been rapacious in killing people and carrying out much of the mayhem in the country with impunity. They stayed away and thereby whittled down the strength of the national dialogue.[11]

The leaders declined the invitation over the inclusion of Miyetti Allah to the roundtable describing it as "a grave insult" to them. This was contained in a letter titled: Re: Roundtable on National Issues and Security and signed by Chief E.K Clark (PANDEF leader), Chief Ayo Adebanjo (Afenifere leader), Chief John Nwodo (President, Ohanaeze) and Dr. Pogu Bitrus (President, Middle Belt Forum). These leaders objected to the sharing of a Roundtable platform with Miyetti Allah – trade association, which for them, should be meeting with their counterparts like Fishermen and Farmers Associations etc., and not leaders of nationalities that make up Nigeria. Though that was not the stated intention of General Abdulsalami Abubakar, they saw the Roundtable as falling in line with the categorization of their respective socio-cultural platforms with Miyetti Allah as reportedly done by Presidential Spokesman, Garba Shehu. They stated: "We consider the above a grave insult on our bodies and our coming to a roundtable with the group would mean acquiescence to the narrative that put us in the same bracket with those wielding illegal AK-47 all over the country and inflicting terror on fellow citizens…Even if the above was not the case with Miyetti Allah, bringing a trade group like them in the same vehicle with the nationalities' organisations would not have been appropriate as there are organisations of their category for fishermen, farmers, spare parts dealers, and poultry owners among others across Nigeria who are not invited. Towards this end, we decline participation in the roundtable as scheduled without prejudice to your peacebuilding effort which is appreciated".

Nonetheless, the meeting was attended by roughly 50 eminent Nigerians, including traditional rulers, leaders of some nationalities,

---

[11]The author participated at this Roundtable and benefitted from a close relationship with the organizers.

serving and retired Security forces/services leaders, politicians, academia, civil society etc.

Despite the staying away by major leaders of some nationalities, the meeting remained very worthwhile. That it took place was a significant buttress on the cries of another former President, Olusegun Obasanjo, who had stressed the need for dialogue but who was being derided by the same government of President Buhari that had, as a result of ill-conceived policies, abhorrent nepotism, impunity and condoning of corruption driven up the temperature of instability in Nigeria.

Prof. Ibrahim Agboola Gambari who chaired the meeting noted that we were at General Abdulsalami Abubakar's Maizube Farms because something is not right in our dear land. Sharing his wealth of experience, he noted that we cannot have a military solution and that we have no alternative to dialogue. In having dialogue, we must build common grounds as well as operate with peacebuilding actions to reinforce other conflict control measures as a way to avoid things falling apart. Prof. Gambari went further to charge the meeting to come up with recommendations on who to do what and when, i.e., we should provide timelines to timely actions meant to address our current downward spiral. Many other leaders like Prof. Bolaji Akinyemi called on the federal government to revisit the outcome document of the 2014 national conference and enact several aspects into law for good governance. Prof. Ango Abdullahi was very positive in emphasizing that crisis of poverty, inequities in various strata of society, unemployment, discriminatory policies of government etc were drivers of the conflict facing Nigeria. He called for the rule of law: a situation in which law is for all.

Of course, the issue of herdsmen and farmers got eloquently put on the table by a leader of one of the many cattle associations, Alhaji Sale Bayari, who claimed to know so much about many things, including

25

movements of weapons from Libya through the Sahel into the hands of herders in Nigeria. Curiously he justified the herders having the weapons because it was a reaction to a persecution complex they face in Nigeria. He literally threatened the rest of Nigerians that if they do not allow the herders to continue to move their cattle as they have been doing over the ages, then they would most likely join the Islamic State, West African Province, against their fatherland. To change this life style, he called for billions of dollars of support, creation of a livestock ministry, (at least he did not ask for a cow ministry), paid training visits for herders to many countries etc and gradual process of change over the next 15 years during which period, the current arrangement needs to continue, etc.

This spokesperson got adequate response. For sure, this was no longer the nineteenth century. Ambassador Joe Keshi rightly and boldly made it clear that we could not be talking of cattle routes in the 21st century. He argued that building a new capital in Abuja as well as other human developmental expansions meant disruptions to cattle routes. So, cattle herders need to adapt and move on to a higher level. Ambassador Keshi elaborated on some of these possibilities drawing from the experience of many countries that produce so much in cattle and dairy products. He expressed the hope that cattle owners would allow herders to change their ways of life for more rewarding modern methods that would free them from the servitude that herders face in the hands of owners.

Drawing from his UN experience which had involved detailing the movements of small arms, General Ishola Williams debunked the claim of weapons moving into the hands of herders from Libya. In some countries, herders carry AK-47 to handle cattle rustling. Have we looked into practices in our neighbouring countries to the north for who desertification has meant crossing through our porous borders into Nigeria to graze? Many of these as bandits are being heard by those claiming to be victims as conversing in French. And in any case, if former Governor Ibikunle Amosun surrendered 1000 AK-47 and million rounds of ammunition as he left office, it shows that it is easy to build a balance of terror as counter moves to compatriots who think only they alone have access to illicit weapons. General Williams countering the bluff of the herders' spokesperson need not look at former Governor Amosun and his surrendered weapons only. Movements that sought more resource allocation in the Niger Delta had weapons that matched Nigerian armed forces in sophistication until late President Yar'Adua opted for negotiations.

Many ethnic groups who are feeling persecuted and they are not threatening to join enemies of Nigeria. This meeting showed the need for another dialogue between crop farmers' associations and herders associations as well as those in aquaculture to work out how to meet Nigeria's food security needs and export without accentuating general insecurity as is the case today. In this regard, recommendations in the books on mechanisms to immediately attend to losses on all sides as they happen, could be looked into.

It is wrong to ethnicize any production arrangement in a multi-ethnic country like Nigeria. Subsidizing food production is understandable. But to do so naming any ethnic group is patently wrong. Ranching or whatever it may be called is no longer rocket science. There was a 12-minute video by Prof. Adewumi Taiwo in Yoruba. He suggested that the first ranch in Nigeria was in Fashola near Oyo that was set up in 1946. This beginning was boosted by Chief Obafemi Awolowo after well researched importation of adaptable "ndama" cattle from Mali with grandparent stocks producing parent stocks and then consumption stocks which were distributed to other farms in Ikorodu, Odeda, Iwo-Oloba, Onise-Ire etc to produce 500 kg succulent cows as opposed to the 250 kg ones being sold currently. These imported breeds of cattle were resistant to trypanosomiasis carried by tsetse fly. They were kept in

27

composite farms that ran for miles. The farms produced grass for cattle, had watering holes and feeds for poultry, pigs and of course cattle. For him, the military ate those cattle up without bothering on producing replacements. According to General Akinrinade at Maizube Farms, for some reasons, all these farms have not been encroached upon. So, what's stopping Governors from the reactivation of such places in their respective states in the whole country? Why can't those who do not have do the same in their states and there by create employment?

According to General Ishola Williams, the EU funded an elaborate ranching arrangement in Yobe about 10 years ago. It was abandoned. He also wondered about why Nigeria cannot follow and support the leads of Sokoto and Zamfara States and Governor Ganduje in Kano who recently called for a ban on rearing cattle along the road from Chad, Niger through Northern Nigeria to Lagos. If President Buhari's government were to simply announce that there would be no forced cattle colonies or settlements or Ruga instead of talking of suspension of the latter, a major tension and second guessing as well as arms race would evaporate leaving the need to address banditry.

As a participant, in my interventions, I was concerned about the impact of corruption on insecurity in Nigeria. I suggested that in addressing banditry, it should not be another design to steal. If we abandoned CCTV for the whole of Abuja with Chinese equipment for that purpose on the ground with the rest of the money stolen, how can any sane person want to have CCTV and drones covering Nigeria's forests as the answer to the banditry Nigeria is facing on its highways? Sounds like the rumour making the round that someone wants to rebuild Murtala Mohammed Airport from scratch by dynamiting what is on ground now as the terminal is moved into the Stella Oduah one that was "completed" but not used in the last two and a half years or so since contract for the access road was only awarded after.

28

The problems of leadership failure and governance was diplomatically put on the table at Maizube Farms. However, in my contributions, I suggested that there is no doubt that leadership failure in Nigeria has resulted in a pandemic culture of corruption that has fueled instability and lack of safety in our lands. How can anyone pretend that more allocation of resources to the armed forces and services was the problem? A National Security Adviser was alleged to have shared $2.1 billion meant for procurement of weapons amongst his friends. Some who returned their share in plea bargains at the beginning of the Buhari administration must be regretting that they did so as they can see many indicted thieves being absorbed into the ruling party and rewarded with Ministerial appointments by President Buhari. It was documented in Court that a service Chief collected about a million and a half dollars every month and pocketed same.

The problems that Prof. Ango Abdullahi and others rightly raised, are results of corruption in our national lives. I recently, looked at President Buhari's Government and corruption and noted the President's tolerance for impunity as he keeps mum when speedy actions were/are needed, and many in the country reading him (rightly or wrongly), as being nepotistic and selective on justice have fueled national fears and general insecurity.

The communique had acceptable recommendations towards handling the problem of insecurity and political instability. It was widely shared with the media. Though General Alani Akinrinade and Brigadier Anthony Ukpo, who jointly steered the group I participated in asked me to write a short paragraph with recommendation on corruption, and I complied but the rapporteuring edited any mention of corruption out of the communique. I was not surprised. The women at the meeting were dissatisfied that the role of women in the avoidance of insecurity that was loudly raised was absent in the communique. In spite of these

29

lacuna, the Roundtable was well worth it.

However, the minimal recommendations of the Roundtable are far from being implemented. Importantly, herders-farmers clashes as well as banditry continued unabated. It was after this meeting that Mrs. Olakunrin was gunned down and a Court of Appeal's police security detail was gunned down and she kidnapped for ransom.

Chapter Four

State Governments' Institutional Responses

Various Nigerian state governments and communities woke up to the reality that the federal government lacks the capacity to provide them security. Growing insecurities without matching commitment from the government, an increasingly overwhelmed and ill-equipped Nigerian Police Force, necessitated the adoption of extra measures. Different communities resorted to self-help strategies. Various grass roots community efforts at vigilantism that did not involve any level of government dot the history of Nigeria.

Perhaps the Hisbah police, that accompanied the operationalization of the criminal aspects of Sharia law in northern Nigeria may be the first formal institutional response on security that set the records straight that security is not and cannot be the preserve of the centralized federal government of Nigeria. Hisbah Vigilante group was set up in 2000 in Zamfara and Kano states, mainly as a result of the Federal Police refusal to carry out arrests on the criminal aspects of the Sharia in a secular State. Following cases of extrajudicial killings, legislative approach started in 2003, with laws being passed to regulate the Hisbah.

Hisbah, an Arabic word meaning an act performed for the good of the society, is an Islamic religious concept that calls for doing what is right and forbidding what is wrong in guiding every Muslim. Hisbah police, in the context of Sharia law, applies to the twelve Muslim dominant states of Kano, Zamfara, Sokoto, Kebbi, Niger, Katsina, Kaduna,

Bauchi, Yobe, Borno, Gombe and Jigawa. The Hisbah Corps, which operates under the jurisdiction of a Hisbah Board comprised of government officials, secular police officers, and religious leaders, is highly decentralized with local units supervised by committees composed of officials and citizens in the communities in which they operate. There are variations among them. Some like in Kano and Zamfara are based on state law and are funded by the state and some lack legal backing.

The Federal government continues to keep quiet on challenging the constitutionality of any portion of Nigeria being under a separate and additional criminal law beyond the penal code. Nigeria's Constitution knows Sharia law and gives it equality with Customary law, i.e, focus is on the private affairs of individuals. Of course, Hisbah continues to be in operation. They are expected to complement the police by informing when necessary leaving the police with arrests. But they do more in practice.

The Hisbah Corps does not have authority to execute arrests and officers are expected to be armed only with non-lethal weapons for self-defense, such as batons. Hisbah officers who observe violations of Sharia are expected to alert the Nigeria Police Force. Other duties of the Hisbah Corps include arbitrating the voluntary reconciliation of disputes, verbally chastising violators of Sharia, and maintaining order at religious celebrations. Hisbah are also trained to assist with disaster response operations.[1]

According to Femi Falana, SAN, Hisbah faced some harrowing attacks by the Federal Government, under President Olusegun Obasanjo in 2003. Even though Hisbah was established in Kano state, (Law No.4 of 2003) with the Kano State Hisbah Corps run by the state

---

[1] Sharia Implementation in Northern Nigeria Over 15 Years. Policy Brief No.2 The Case of Hisbah

government, taking effect in 2003, the Federal Government said it was illegal.[2] In a letter addressed to the Kano State Government, President Olusegun Obasanjo expressed concerns over the constitutionality of Hisbah, putting up a fact finding mission on the issue.

What Kano's Hisbah advocates were after was a Supreme Court ruling that would declare Hisbah lawful, and restrain the Inspector-General of Police from interfering in and disrupting the full implementation of the Law.

However, the Supreme Court ruled on March 2, 2007 that the case did not come under its jurisdiction as the Kano State Attorney-General's complaints were against the Inspector-General of Police and not against the Federation. Seven Supreme Court Justices were unanimous on this and the case was struck out.[3] In his judgment, Umaru Atu Kalgo JSC further elucidated the inaction of the Federal Government, arguing that the President of the Federation only wrote a letter and sent a delegation on a fact-finding mission. He did not take or threaten any action against Kano state or any of the operators of the Hisbah law.

It is clear that the Federal Government has never challenged the legality of enforcing the criminal aspects of Shari'ah or Hisbah in the Supreme Court. Nor has it ever interfered with Shari'ah implementation under a secular Constitution. The Inspector-General of Police had acted in his own capacity when he made the claim that the Hisbah Corps was unconstitutional. The plaintiff's complaints were not against the Federation and so the Supreme Court had no original jurisdiction. The plaintiff was left with the option of taking the complaint to the Federal High Court.

On March 29, 2007 the Daily Triumph reported that the presiding judge of the Abuja Court of Appeal, Justice Babs Kuewumi, ruled the detention of the Chairman of the Hisbah Corps, Yahaya Faruk Chedi, and his deputy, Abubakar Rabo Abdulkareen to be unlawful and ordered the Federal Government pay each of them the sum of N500,000 as compensation for their illegal detention.[4] In effect, Hisbah Corps have been operating successfully in the 12 northern states.

The relationship between the Hisbah Corps and civil police has been sometimes acrimonious. The Nigeria Police Force (NPF), to whom the Hisbah must report crimes, frequently refuse to cooperate in enforcement of religious law. On multiple occasions, NPF officers have arrested Hisbah members for trespassing when the latter had attempted to enter private property to enforce Sharia. But recently, Hisbah Commission in Zamfara state reportedly arrested a male civil police official for being found in the company of three women at a hotel in Gusau, Zamfara state. The manager of the Hotel was also arrested.[5]

Plateau State, under Governor Jonah Jang collaborated with the Federal government and was assisted by the UN, to set up Operation Rainbow as a civil-military complementary arrangement that was aimed at minimizing insecurity in the State. Though criticized he continued till he left office with his successor showing less interest.

Even the Federal government itself contracted private companies to form pipeline surveillance security entities to reduce sabotage on the lifeline of Nigeria: petroleum oil and gas transported through pipelines.

The increasing weight of security challenges on the corporate existence of Nigeria, coupled with gross inadequate manpower at the country's security agencies, especially at the Nigerian Police Force, has resulted in a new innovation, for collaboration and synergy among security actors,

---

[2]Operation Amotekun: Govs meet Osinbajo, to back exercise with law. Punch News, 23rd January, 2020.
[3]Nigeria: The Battle for Shari'ah Supremacy, International Institute for Religious Freedom.
https://www.iirf.eu/articles/iirf-research-writer/nigeria-the-battle-for-shariah-supremacy/
[4]Ibid.
[5]Guardian news, December 30, 2019

popularly referred to as the Joint Task Forces (JTFs) a flexible arrangement (on as needed basis), set up for specific purposes and assignments to resolve different security concerns.[6] JTFs are usually set up based on the principle of inter-agency collaboration, meaning that all the security groups would formally work together to achieve specific integrated mandates.[7] For example, the JTF in the Niger Delta is set up to checkmate militancy in the area, the Special Task Force (STF) in Plateau State is set up to curb ethno-religious conflicts in the state.[8]

In Borno State, many outfits were created by the state government and saddled with security duties, especially in the wake of Boko Haram insurgency. Aside from the local Hisbah Corps, there is also the Civilian Joint Task Force (CJTF) created under the last administration called BOYES (Borno Youth Volunteers).[9] They work in collaboration with the military to fight Boko Haram. Also working for the security of the state are local hunters and vigilante groups, which have been around even before insurgency. Recently, the Borno state Governor, Prof. Babagana Zulum, employed the services of hunters from across the north and neighbouring countries to boost the efforts at fighting insurgency and criminality. All these groups carry light arms, like locally made and pomp action guns.[10]

---

[6]Mathias Daji Yake, "Military Joint Task Force and the Challenges of Internal Security Operations in Nigeria: The Plateau State Experience" in Oshita O. Oshita et. al., (eds), Internal Security Management in Nigeria (London: Palgrave Macmillan, 2019), pp. 441-459.
[7]Ibid.
[8]Ibid.
[9]On this, and more please see a detailed report in https://www.thisdaylive.com/index.php/2020/01/13/23-states-run-local-security-outfits-as-groups-demand-decentralised-policing/
[10]Ibid

Chapter Five

Operation Amotekun

In the light of the security challenges in the Southwest, some of which were detailed in Chapter One, the six Governors of the Southwest met in June 2019 with stake holders on the recurrent spate of insecurity in Western Nigeria.[1] This meeting could be suggested as setting the stage for the launching of "Operation Amotekun". The meeting was attended by the six governors: Dr. Kayode Fayemi (Ekiti), Mr. Seyi Makinde (Oyo), Mr. Babajide Sanwo-Olu (Lagos), Prince Dapo Abiodun (Ogun), Ogbeni Oluwarotimi Akeredolu (Ondo) and Gboyega Oyetola (Osun) were in attendance. The meeting was reportedly organized by the Development Agenda for Western Nigeria (DAWN) Commission in Ibadan. They took far-reaching decisions, including the formation of a collaborative security network for the Southwest geopolitical zone. It was agreed that Governor Akeredolu would be the Convener with his Oyo state counterpart, Governor Makinde as host with active support from the Development Agenda for Western Nigeria (DAWN) Commission.[2]

Popular interests and concerns were also a source of pressure on the governors who were appearing impotent like the federal government. Insinuations on political ambitions of some of the governors or their

---

[1]https://www.thisdaylive.com/index.php/2019/06/23/ahead-of-security-summit-yoruba-elders-set-agenda-for-swest-governors/
[2]Ibid

godfathers were being discussed as explanations for why the leadership were quiet on the grazing of cattle over farmlands as well as banditry.

At the same time, traditional authorities also canvassed strongly on the need to send criminally minded herders and bandits out of the Southwest. The Ooni of Ife, Oba Adeyeye Ogunwusi took the lead in pushing for a Southwest complementary security apparatus.

Stephen Banji Akintoye, Emeritus Professor of History and leader of the Yorubas has been vociferous on the deterioration of security in Nigeria in general and with respect to the Southwest geopolitical zone in particular. For him, the Yoruba nation faces a plethora of developmental crisis but none of these is as crucial as what he describes as the sustained invasion of the Yoruba homeland since 2014, by gangs of Fulani herdsmen and militias. This onslaught, he states, has been characterized by destruction of farms, killing of large numbers of farmers and their family members, raping and killing women, destroying villages, kidnapping people, and generally engaging in uttermost rampage in various parts of Yorubaland, as the most critical challenge crying for urgent attention, in other to effectively address other developmental challenges.

Like President Olusegun Obasanjo, Prof Akintoye, considers a thorough understanding of the causes of the rampage very critical in addressing it. Beyond the positions of it being a sharp contest between farmers and herders, in response to competition over farming and grazing lands, which is also accentuated by desertification, he suggests that, there is a Secret Agenda to skillfully remake Nigeria by the Fulani. To achieve this feat, he thinks, is the explanation behind the massive free and unrestrained entry of Fulanis from the West African region into Nigeria, especially with the position that Nigeria is a divinely made home for the Fulanis. He states that the domination of the political space in Nigeria by Fulanis since the pre-colonial era till date is in some sync with this indoctrination. He argues that these positions, are not falsely being made, but are being articulated by the Fulani themselves, especially their elites.[3]

He regularly points to the situation in Benue state in support of his reasoning. There the Government of Ortom had in 2017 institutionalized a system to limit the activities of cattle herders in the state as a way of checking the killings. But this met with a greater threat, and actual implementation of the threats resulting in the lives of 73 and massive destructions in the January 1, 2018 incident and others that followed.

Prof. Akintoye states that since 2014, almost all parts of the country, have been seeing the activities of ill-minded arm bearing Fulani groups, in some tactics of occupying the whole territory. The activities became more pronounced and targeted at the Southwest as from 2015, starting with the experience of Chief Olu Falae. The attacks grew from highway robbery and kidnapping of targeted individuals for ransom, to destruction of farms and disruption of economics activities.

He considers the climax of the monstrous activities of the Fulanis in the Southwest, to be the issuance of threat to the Yoruba nation, following a law in Oyo state to limit Fulani presence.

In addressing the issue, he called for a general awareness across different groups of the challenge at hand, especially in learning from cases in Benue State and elsewhere. For him, the government must also proactively resurrect pre-existing indigenous security arrangements such as the OPC, and others for greater security. He constantly argue that there is no better time for the numerous Yoruba socio-cultural and

---

[3] All information from the speech was coined from The Task Before Our Yoruba Nation Today By Professor Banji Akintoye By NationalInsight. November 18, 2019
https://nationalinsightnews.com/the-task-before-our-yoruba-nation-today-by-professor-banji-akintoye/

self-determination groups to come together in the defense of their land, than now. A more logical and peaceful approach, he suggests, would be to place a demand on the Fulani to halt their agenda, thereafter, the country should seat at the restructuring table.

With all the pressures on the Governors of the Southwest geopolitical zone, it was not a surprise when on Thursday January 9, 2020 the leaders of the six Southwest states (Lagos, Ogun, Oyo, Osun, Ekiti and Ondo) launched the popularly hailed and appreciated Operation Amotekun with a lot of fanfare.

At the launching, Governor Kayode Fayemi, of Ekiti State stated: ,"Amotekun is a complement that will give our people confidence that they are being looked after by those they elected into office. So, we do not want this to create fear in the mind of anybody as we are not creating a regional police force and are fully aware of the steps we must take to have state police. We do not want anybody to misconstrue the concept of Amotekun....As elected leaders, our primary responsibility, according to Section 14 (2) of the Nigerian Constitution 1999 as amended, is the security and welfare of citizens. That was what informed the governors coming together to fashion out a way to complement the work of the mainstream security agencies overstretched in their efforts to arrest the menace that have afflicted the entire country."[4]

The new year's surprise, may not be much of a big news to many, as this development, is a culmination of strategic security summits held in the latter part of 2019, in the interest of the security of lives and properties of the peoples of the Southwest geo-political zone. This comes against the background of the many cases of killings, kidnappings and other security threats that the region had faced. Operation Amotekun, which

---

[4]Govement of Ekiti State website, AMOTEKUN NOT REGIONAL POLICE - FAYEMI.
https://ekitistate.gov.ng/amotekun-not-regional-police-fayemi/
See also, PM News report, Operation Amotekun: Western Nigeria governors launch Security outfit. 9/01/2020

was also seen as community effort to policing, as described by the Governors present, is a child born out of necessity, to attend to the security challenges in the zone, whilst working closely with the Federal Police. Highlight of the event, which was attended by all governors of the south west states, except Dapo Abiodun of Ogun state, Gboyega Oyetola of Osun and Babajide Sanwo-Olu of Lagos state, saw the contributions of patrol vehicles, motor cars and motor cycles by each of the states. This development, more than any other, has kept the country very engaged since the start of the year. Interestingly, it has sparked fundamental questions on issues affecting the soul of the country.

The Nigerian Police Force and other security agencies that were invited did not attend the ceremony. The military and police leadership at the Southwest geo-political zone did not attend. They claimed they did not receive instructions to attend from Abuja.

While the military claimed not to have been consulted, there was consultation between the governors and the Nigerian Police Force. On Monday, September 2, 2019, for instance, the Inspector General of Police Mohammed Adamu attended the Southwest geopolitical zone security summit at the International Conference Centre, University of Ibadan. At this meeting, the IGP briefed the Governors of Oyo and Osun states as well as Deputy-Governors from the other four states on the force's desire to boost Operation Puff Adder, including through partnership with Oodua People's Congress and others working towards a secured Southwest.[5]

The day before the launching of Operation Amotekun, Governor Fayemi, was guest of the IGP in Abuja for a meeting to sort out all grey areas. The IGP had requested to meet all the governors, but they sent Fayemi to represent them. The IGP reportedly agreed after the handling

---

[5]Ola Ajayi and Deola Badru, Insecurity: IGP, South West governors approve deployment of Special Forces, September 3, 2019 in the Vanguard.

of grey areas. He saw the development as an outcome of the security summit of September 2, 2019.[6] Asked to confirm whether the IGP approved that Operation Amotekun be launched, the spokesman of the Nigeria Police Force, Deputy Commissioner of Police, Frank Mba, stated that the police boss was not opposed to Operation Amotekun only that he wanted it to comply with the national security policy.[7]

The increasing nature of the indices of insecurity in the country is not only disturbing it also questions the effectiveness of the Nigerian security architecture, especially with respect to the Nigerian Police Force which is primarily saddled with the responsibility of providing security to the people.[8]

In addition, it signifies a need to be open-minded and think out of the box on how to secure lives and properties in Nigeria. Perhaps it is time to put on Deng Xiaoping's thinking, if we consider the security of all Nigerians as critical. For him, "it does not matter whether a cat is black or white as long as it catches mice."[9]

There have been debates and arguments on how best to reform the Nigerian Police and its operations (for effective security) which often goes with calls for restructuring of not just the national security architecture but the country itself. We need not engage in a discussion of the whole scale restructuring of Nigeria but state clearly that there is the need to focus on a restructuring of Nigeria's security architecture.

The calls for Community Policing to bring about some level of decentralization of the responsibility of policing to the States and Local

[6]https://allafrica.com/stories/202001090340.html
[7]Ibid.
[8]Adebola Rafiu Bakare & Gabriel Temitope Aderinola, The Nigeria Police and Internal Security Management in Nigeria, in Oshita O. Oshita et. al., (eds), Internal Security Management in Nigeria (London: Palgrave Macmillan, 2019), pp 461-483.
[9]https://quotes.thefamouspeople.com/deng-xiaoping-4263.php

government level has been ongoing. In the two-fold argument, some more conservative positions consider it best to stick to the Federal Police as bequeathed by the erstwhile military rulers of Nigeria, basing their argument on the potential abuse and exploitation of State Police by power thirsty elements in authority. Others think the excessive centralization of the Police, such that orders are received from Abuja, before critical decisions could be arrived at, on issues bothering on security in the remote villages, where there are sometimes, near absence of police presence, is inefficient, hence the need for State policing arrangement, to brings policing closer to the grass roots. Furthermore, abuse must not be seen as limited to lower levels of governance. The Federal government could also mis-use centralized policing arrangement.

The arguments for and against State Police, is also not new in the legislature. Ike Ekweremadu, a long serving member of the Senate, had at various fora in the past spoken about the need for the establishment of State Police to complement the Federal government's efforts towards stemming the security challenges facing the nation. For instance, as Deputy Senate President in the Eighth Senate while reacting to the June 2018 sacking of 11 Plateau State communities by suspected armed herdsmen resulting in the loss of over 100 lives, Ekweremadu, put the blame squarely on unitary policing, which he described as a misnomer in modern policing especially in federal states.[10]

Subsequently, an Ekweremadu-led Committee on the Constitution came up with a constitution amendment bill for state police. "The Constitution Amendment Bill to Provide for the Establishment of State Police and Other Related Matters 2018" sponsored by Ekweremadu and 74 other members of the Committee on Constitution Review was

---

10 Of Tinubu's Stand On Amotekun and Ekweremadu's Bill on State Police
January 26, 2020. This Day News

consequently accorded First Reading in April, 2018.[11] According to the Bill, the State Police, shall be organised and administered in accordance with such provisions as may be prescribed by a Law of the House of Assembly of a State, but subject to the framework and guidelines established by an Act of the National Assembly.

To address the fear of abuse expressed by opponents of State Police in the present dispensation, the Bill provides that the Commissioner of Police of a State shall be appointed by the Governor of the state on the advice of the National Police Service Commission, subject to confirmation of such appointment by the House of Assembly of the State and shall be in office for a period of five years only or until he attains a retirement age prescribed by law, whichever is earlier.

Senator Dino Melaye, in his contribution was vehemently against the creation of state police because it would be abused by the governors.[12] He made some very critical points, which boiled down to the need for some changes and initiatives on the Police Force. He called for effective information gathering, which has suffered following the loss of confidence between the citizens and the Police. Nigerian citizens no longer have confidence in security agencies to the extent that they hoard information. How best do citizens share information, with a Police that is nearly inaccessible? For example, how much help could be rendered to a Police Officer that barely understands the terrain or area he/she was posted to from the Police Headquarters in Abuja? How best could he/she relate with the people for information sharing?

With several state initiatives and community self-help initiatives and vigilante groups, can we confidently, say State Policing is not in operation already? Are the people not taking up the full responsibility of securing themselves?

---

[11]Ibid.
[12]Ibid.

With the launching of Operation Amotekun, many strident calls are being made on the need to restructure the Nigerian security architecture. Doyin Okupe advised on the need to "align with modernity and civilization".[13] For him, it would be better to take the bull by the horn, in implementing State Policing as a panacea to the security issues, and a better national option against creating a motely web of mushroom, primitive, and unstandardized local security outfits nationwide.[14] On January 26, the Coalition of Northern Groups (CNG) announced the floating of "Shege Ka Fasa" a security outfit for the region. The Middle Belt Forum, while urging governors to face head-on security issues in the region, would also like to replicate 'Operation Amotekun' in the Middle Belt.[15]

In conclusion, what is important, is the need for the government to respond to change. All pointers clearly show that the Federal Police arrangement has not done so much over the years. To continue to fear trying a different idea, only because of potential threats, which could be mitigated, is cowardly. There is urgent need to innovate the security architecture, such that there is a decentralization that allows for the government and the people at the state and local levels to be heavily involved and carried along on their security, in the context that relates well to them.

---

[13] John Owen Nwachukwu, Amotekun: Doyin Okupe sends message to Osinbajo on security outfit. January 25, 2020 in Daily Post report.
[14] Ibid.
[15] AMOTEKUN: We're considering similar outfit — Middle Belt ON JANUARY 16, https://www.vanguardngr.com/2020/01/amotekun-were-considering-similar-outfit-m-belt/ By Dayo Johnson, Dapo Akinrefon et al.

Chapter Six

Popular Welcome for Operation Amotekun and Minor Irritations

Traditional media and social media went agog with the launching of Operation Amotekun. This was much the case in the Southwest geopolitical zone. It had been long that the whole geopolitical zone was united on any issue. There was no quivering. Even reluctant leadership voices and those in the Southwest that initially dilly-dallied ended up welcoming the development with suggestions on how to improve further. They were dragged along by the popular reactions that accompanied the launching ceremony.

However, Abubakar Malami (SAN), the Attorney-General of the Federation, through one Dr. Umar Gwandu, his Special Assistant on Media and Public relations intervened with a killjoy press statement that is reproduced below:

Press Release on the Paramilitary Organisation named "Amotekun"

Federal Republic of Nigeria is a sovereign entity and is governed by laws meant to sustain its corporate existence as a constitutional democracy. It is a Federation of states, but with the Federal Government superintending over matters of national interests.

The division of executive and legislative authority between the Federal and State Governments has been clearly defined by the

Constitution of the Federal Republic of Nigeria 1999 (as amended).

It is against the same background that matters relating to the peace, order and good government of the Federation and in particular, the defence of the country, are enshrined in the Exclusive Legislative List.

The Second Schedule in Item 17 deals with defence. This is a matter that is within the exclusive operational competence of the Federal of Government of Nigeria. No other authority at the state level, whether the executive or legislature has the legal authority over defence.

The setting up of the paramilitary organization called "Amotekun" is illegal and runs contrary to the provisions of the Nigerian law.

The Constitution of the Federal Republic of Nigeria 1999 (as amended) has established the Army, Navy and Airforce, including the Police and other numerous paramilitary organisations for the purpose of the defence of Nigeria.

As a consequence of this, no State Government, whether singly or in a group has the legal right and competence to establish any form of organization or agency for the defence of Nigeria or any of its constituent parts.

This is sanctioned by the provision of Item 45 of the Second Schedule of the Constitution of the Federal Republic of Nigeria (as amended) authorizing the Police and other Federal government security services established by law to maintain law and order.

The law will take its natural course in relation to excesses

46

associated with organization, administration and participation in "Amotekun" or continuous association with it as an association.

Finally, it is important to put on record that the Office of the Attorney General and Minister of Justice was not consulted on the matter. If it had, proper information and guidance would have been offered to ensure that Nigeria's defense and corporate entity are preserved at all times.

There were several reactions from all over the country to the press statement. Overwhelmingly, the Attorney-General was taken to task on the legal issues he raised. Political dimensions of such an attempt to throw a wet blanket over the hope of building a more secure environment by states and geopolitical zones were also brought up. Minor voices from Northern Nigeria like those of Miyetti Allah supported the position of the Attorney-General.

Two of the major reactions came from two Senior Advocates of Nigeria: Femi Falana and Ebun Adegboruwa.

Human rights activist, Femi Falana (SAN) in his reaction, captured across various news media, retorted that the Police was effectively carried along during the process of preparation for Amotekun, especially with the Inspector-General of Police, Mr. Mohammed Adamu meeting with the Southwest governors represented by Gov Kayode Fayemi of Ekiti State. The subsequent endorsing of the security initiative by the Police, means that the government is also in support. Therefore, the statement of the Attorney-General of the Federal Government that he was not consulted before the establishment of Amotekun is totally uncalled for and ought to be ignored by the Southwest governors.

47

Falana, paid attention to the application of the word, "Government" under the Nigerian Constitution. The word Government, as contained in section 318 of the Constitution is said to include the Government of the Federation, or any State, or of a local government council or any person who exercises power or authority on its behalf.

Mr Malami's purported proscription of Amotekun is hypocritical and discriminatory on the basis of the existence of similar security structures, like the Civilian JTF in Yobe and Borno states with 26,000 well-armed volunteers who have been assisting the armed forces to combat terrorism in the Northeast region. Hisbah in Kano and Zamfara states. The Lagos State government has equally established the Neighbourhood Watch to assist the Police and other security agencies in protecting the life and property of every person living in Lagos.

By virtue of section 214 of the Constitution, only one police force should operate in Nigeria. The establishment of other state security agencies, like the Civil Defense is nothing but a constitutional breach. The establishment and arming of other security agencies as the State Security Service (SSS), the Economic and Financial Crimes Commission, the Independent Corrupt Practices and Offences Commission, Nigeria Customs Service, Nigeria Correctional Service and other paramilitary agencies takes away the right of the government to stop any state from setting up a security outfit.

Critically assessing section 227 of the Constitution, from where the AGF hinged his argument, Falana argues that the Constitution has not prohibited the establishment of security outfits for the defense of the people of Nigeria. While calling on Mr. Malami to take up the issue before the Supreme Court, he advised the governments of Ekiti, Ondo, Osun, Ogun and Oyo states to ignore Mr. Malami's purported proscription and proceed to enact the necessary laws similar to the Neighbourhood Watch Law of Lagos State.[1]

In a similar vein, Mr. Ebun Adegboruwa (SAN), observed that the Operation Amotekun development has demonstrated the capacity of Nigerians to organize for social change. Critically interpreting the provision of section 14 (2) (b) of the 1999 Constitution, he reiterated that it is the primary duty of responsible governments, the world over, to protect the lives and properties of citizens. Any government like as seen in Nigeria, that fails in this responsibility, is not worth its salt. He cited the cases of Boko Haram, and other forms of insecurities, that have also threatened the lives of the "high and mighty" even in public service, with the example of the kidnapped Justice of the Court Appeal in Edo state in broad day light.[2]

For him, Section 214 of the Constitution only established the Nigeria Police Force without specifying its powers or granting it any exclusivity in criminal matters. There is no exclusivity granted to the Nigeria Police Force in relation to safety of lives and property. What the Constitution has prohibited in section 214 is that 'no other police force shall be established for the Federation of Nigeria or any part thereof.' Even though the 1999 Constitution has established the Nigeria Police Force in its section 214, thorough study and investigation will reveal that the Nigeria Police Force was long established under section 3 of the Police Act of 1943, when the colonialists NEVER had in mind the idea of exclusivity. Even after independence, regions had their own police.

For Adegboruwa, the interpretation of Section 214, is purely an issue of nomenclature. Under section 214 of the Constitution, the name and nomenclature of The Nigeria Police Force is unique and exclusive and no other entity can be established in Nigeria or any part of it, with the same NAME. Any other name, Hisbah, Amotekun, JTF can exist.[3]

---

[1] Femi Falana (SAN) in a press statement, reacting to Malami's position on operation Amotekun. Premium Times on January 15, 2020 captured it in "Amotekun not illegal—Falana.
[2] Bridget Edokwe, The Legality of Amotekun, by Ebun-Olu Adegboruwa, SAN. In BarristerNG.com
[3] Ibid.

Any state could, on as needed bases, establish security agencies, so long as it is not called the Police. The examples of the establishment of the Nigerian Security and Civil Defence Corps and Lagos State Neighborhood Watch, and the passage of the bill for Peace Corps as well as the existence of similar security outfits in some states, in the north and elsewhere are clear examples.

The AGF position may have only been a hasty negation to the 2015 APC Manifesto to all Nigerians, promising to 'enable States and Local Governments to employ State and Community Police to address the PECULIAR NEEDS OF EACH COMMUNITY.' Besides, all residential estates across Nigeria have security men helping to gather intelligence and maintain peace. The questions then is this: what is so special about Amotekun that the federal government is sounding jittery?

The series of reactions following the launch of Operation Amotekun, saw pockets of solidarity rallies in the south western states on Tuesday January 21, 2020. Representatives of the various stakeholders, such as the Yoruba Worldwide Congress, hunters union and the OPC, who by design would provide pool for the Amotekun recruits, together with representatives of the National Association of Nigerian Students (NANS) and other groups in the south west region protested the opposition of the federal government to Operation Amotekun.

The groups marched through the streets of the capitals of the states, demanding that the federal government retrace its steps, and that the regional governors remain resolute in pursuing the actualisation of Amotekun.[4]

---

[4] Amotekun: NANS, OPC, hunters, others hold solidarity rallies across Southwest, Premium Times report on January 22, 2020.
https://www.premiumtimesng.com/news/headlines/373847-amotekun-nans-opc-hunters-others-hold-solidarity-rallies-across-southwest.html

There were slight varieties in the nature of the solidarity rallies in the states. In Ado-Ekiti, besides NANS and , other groups such as Vigilante Group of Nigeria, Yoruba Koya, Man 'O War, Oodua Union, Ekiti Council of Elders and Agbekoya were also at the solidarity rally. There was calm, with the Police and SSS available on ground, as the rally connected major points in the state.

In the spirit of unity and solidarity for a passionate course, the groups, and individuals were seen   reacting passionately especially with the reaction from Malami in their respective submissions, held that the Amotekun initiative had berthed permanently in the region and that it was not formed to fight Fulani herders but only the unruly and destructive ones.[10]

In Akure, the Ondo State capital, members of the NANS Zone D, comprising Ondo, Osun, Ekiti, Oyo, Ogun and Lagos states, fronted the rally with reactions against the position of the AGF, which at the time, generated several negative reactions.

In Abeokuta in Ogun State, the Amotekun solidarity rally witnessed a low turnout. But the police and civil defense corps were also seen stationed in strategic locations of the venue, at Rally Square in Panseke area of the town.[11]

In Ogun State, the situation was not so different, with very similar issues and worries raised. There was comparison with the Hisbah and the JTF as basis for criticizing the position of Malami. At Ibadan and Osogbo, reports from news agencies showed very similar pattern, reaffirming strong solidarity and commitment to Amotekun.

However, the situation was different in Lagos, as Armed Policemen, on Tuesday January 21, 2020, aborted the planned rally, by barricading

---

[10]Ibid.
[11]Ibid.

Gani Fawehinmi Park, Ojota, Lagos State, venue of the scheduled pro Amotekun rally, preventing rally enthusiasts from converging on the ground.[12] According to Vanguard newspaper, a senior police officer stated that: "We are acting based on an order that the rally must not hold, because it tends to disrupt the peaceful nature of a state like Lagos."[13]

There were other reactions against the Attorney-General's position. Diaspora Yorubas in North America, otherwise known as Egbe Omo Yoruba, say they welcome the recent launch of a south west security network in Nigeria called Amotekun, and called on "every state assembly in the South-west to urgently pass the enabling laws to validate the establishment of Amotekun as a joint venture of the region,"[14] according to a statement by the president of the association, Durojaiye Akindutire, a medical doctor based in New York.

Citing the challenges of peace, security and order in the region, the association gave kudos to what it called "the foresight of South-west governors and stakeholders including political leaders, traditional rulers and especially DAWN Commission for the initiative,"[15] and claimed that it has brought relief and peace to the region, which was enveloped by "unprecedented heightened state of emergency…in the first ten months of 2018 when kidnappers wrought havoc beyond imagination and citizens' fear for their lives was at the highest point in decades."[16]

The association pointed at the economic loss the state of insecurity in the region has brought as well as the threat to prospective foreign tourists "since even many of the association's members were reluctant to travel home on vacation" and said, for these reasons, they have

---

[12] Lagos police abort pro-Amotekun rally, as Yoruba group insists Amotekun will stand. https://www.vanguardngr.com/2020/01/lagos-police-abort-pro-amotekun-rally-as-yoruba-group-insists-amotekun-ll-stand/
[13] Ibid.
[14] Premium Times, South-West House of Assembly tasked to pass law enabling Amotekun. January 18, 2020
[15] Ibid.
[16] Ibid.

nothing but appreciation for the governors and other stakeholders who pulled off the new security outfit.

Referencing the statement credited to the Attorney-General, Abubakar Malami who, citing legal and constitutional grounds, declared Amotekun illegal, the group said the principal consideration of any legal or constitutional regime is the peace and security of all citizens and asked "if an outfit established for the protection of lives is deemed unconstitutional, we fail to understand the legitimacy of such a Constitution"?[17]

The Egbe Omo Yoruba encouraged South-west governors and stakeholders to hold the fort, arguing that "if Hisbah has been operating since 1999 and it is not deemed unconstitutional, Amotekun has a right to protect the people of Yorubaland from violent marauders who have not been effectively deterred by the existing federal security operatives."[18]

At a meeting of Speakers from the six Southwest state houses of assembly the legislative leaders formally declared support for Operation Amotekun. In attendance were Adebo Ogundoyin (Oyo), Funminiyi Afuye (Ekiti), Bamidele Oleyelogun (Ondo), Timothy Owoeye (Osun), Oluomo Olakunle (Ogun) and Mudashiru Obasa (Lagos). The Southwest Speakers, said that Amotekun is, no doubt, a replica of Hisbah and JTF which have been in operation in the Northern geopolitical zones for many years. In the communique signed and made available to Premium Times on Friday January 25, 2020 they added that Amotekun will go a long way in curbing the security problems facing the Southwest zone.

After an exhaustive deliberation, the conference resolved as follows:

---

[17]Ibid.
[18]Ibid.

That the newly launched Southwest Security Network (a.k.a Operation Amotekun) seeks to complement all the security outfits in the Southwest and not to replace them.

That the establishment of Operation Amotekun in the Southwest is in tandem with spirit of the constitution which make the protection of lives and properties a matter of priority for any responsible government.

That Operation Amotekun is a welcome development, especially in the spirit of existing community policing laws in the South-western states.

That Operation Amotekun is similar to already existing security outfits such as Hisbah and Joint Task Force in the Northern part of the country which had been in operation several years ago.

That the Conference wholeheartedly supports the coming into being of Operation Amotekun, knowing fully well that it will go a long way in curbing the worrisome security problem facing the South-West region.

In a surprise move, various media outlets on January 23, 2020, reported that Abubakar Malami (SAN), the Attorney-General, during a chat with Radio Nigeria, Abuja had changed his position. He reportedly cleared the air on his earlier statement which has since generated series of reactions. He explained that he did not say that Amotekun was illegal. In his words, "I was misinterpreted on Operation Amotekun, I did not say it's illegal. I said the Operation Amotekun should be properly backed by law, so if at the end of this government, if the operation has been backed by law, any government would not rubbish the operation. I said if they failed to enact a law in support of Amotekun in the South-West Region of Nigeria, another government can come and say it's illegal and this is because it is not backed up by any law. So, it is just a piece of advice to the state governors to use their power and the State Houses of

Assembly in their various states to enact a law that will make the operation more effective"[19]

However, on the same day, another discordant tone was issued as a press statement from the office of the Attorney-General and signed by his Assistant on media and public relations, Dr. Umar Gwandu. He insisted that Operation Amotekun is illegal under the Constitution. He shifted the goal post and claimed that Nigeria's Constitution does not recognize any regional security arrangement.[20]

The governors of the six Southwest states sought a meeting with President Buhari over the statement of the Attorney-General of the Federation. With the President being away in the United Kingdom, the governors were received by the Vice-President on January 23, 2020. Also present at the meeting were the Attorney-General of the federation and the Inspector General of Police.

At the end of the meeting both the office of the Vice-President and Governor Akeredolu indicated that the meeting was very successful. Mr. Laolu Akande, the spokesperson to the Vice-President in a statement informed that: "Having regard to the need for all hands to be on deck in addressing the security concerns across the country, it was agreed that the structure of Amotekun should also align with the Community Policing strategy of the Federal Government. It was also agreed that necessary legal instruments will be put in place by each of the States to give legal backing to the initiative and address all issues concerning the regulation of the security structure."

Governor Rotimi Akeredolu spoke to journalists on behalf of all as the Attorney-General who was present decided not to speak. He stated that they would embark on a legal framework to back Amotekun that has

---

[19] Amotekun: I was misquoted, I didn't say it's illegal, says Malami. Punch report on 26, January 2020.
[20] https://punchng.com/malami-insists-amotekun-illegal-says-falanas-u-turn-vindicates-fg

come to stay. In the presence of the Attorney-General, he noted that the Attorney-General had indicated that he was misquoted as saying that Operation Amotekun is illegal. In addition, he clearly stated that there were consultations with the Inspector-General of Police.[21]

Prof. Stephen Banji Akintoye, the Yoruba leader on January 26, 2020 released a video in which he strongly welcomed Operation Amotekun as a structured response to the onslaught of Fulani herders over the last four years. He stated that many of these Fulani herders came from outside of Nigeria with sophisticated weaponry. Asserting that Yorubas were not used to street fights and had always preferred dialogue but in the current circumstances, they are now ready to have well trained Yoruba youths provide security for Yorubaland.

With his passion for the security of Yorubaland, and as the leader of the Yoruba World Congress, it was not surprising to see Prof Akintoye, blowing hot against the federal Attorney-General's dismissal of the newly launched Operation Amotekun as illegal. He charged all Nigerian regions to rise in self-defense, in the spirit of which the Operation Amotekun has come to stay.[22] To this end, he has called on all Yoruba people to support Amotekun, even if it means challenging the federal government in Court, in favour of a course for defense and security of her people.

---

[21] https://www.premiumtimesng.com/news/headlines/374122-federal-govt-south-west-governors-agree-on-amotekun.html
[22] Video: Professor Akintoye blows hot on Amotekun, Fulani
https://www.thenewsnigeria.com.ng/2020/01/26/video-professor-akintoye-blows-hot-on-amotekun-fulani/
The News Sunday, January 26, 2020

Concluding Remarks

Vicious attacks on the Southwest geopolitical zone (a convenient political terminology that has no constitutional status) of Nigeria in 2019 through maiming, kidnapping, killings and theft of property resulted in what is called "Operation Amotekun". Amotekun the Yoruba word for Leopard became the code name for the Western Nigeria Security Network. Under this arrangement, the 6 states of: Lagos, Ogun, Oyo, Osun, Ekiti and Ondo came together to enhance their security in collaboration with the Nigerian security forces.

That the Nigerian security forces are overstretched is not in doubt. The Nigerian military forces are bogged down by Boko Haram in the Northeast geopolitical zone without any clear answer to the problem. The inability to cope resulted in collaboration of the military with civilians in what is called Civilian Joint Task Force that transcends one state in its operations that brought Borno and Yobe states together. Nigeria has no longer been as forthcoming to participate effectively in United Nations peacekeeping operations- a source of corruption for a few Nigerian military and civilian leaders who divert UN payments on equipment and at times entitlements of soldiers. The paucity of capacity of the so called giant of Africa also resulted in an African Union supported multinational joint task force bringing together Nigeria's immediate neighbours to face Boko Haram.

The Buhari government has done better in handling Boko Haram, than its predecessor. This government reduced the capacity of Boko Haram to hold and maintain territory in the Northeast of Nigeria. The spate of sporadic bombings has reasonably reduced. Nonetheless, the problem remains.

The police are understaffed and poorly equipped. During the defence of the security service's 2019 budget as Acting Inspector-General of

Police Mohammed Adamu, before being subsequently confirmed, informed Nigeria that under-staffing was the main problem of the force that manifests in the comical state of the Nigerian Police Force. For him, there was also the problem of under-funding resulting in being under-equipped to fight crime. He pointed out that one police officer to 662 citizens, is grossly inadequate. Comparative figures are: Singapore with a ratio of 1:137; Egypt 1:186; South Africa 1:366; Norway 1: 188; USA 1: 298 and Canada 1:188. The United Nations suggests that the ratio should not be more than 1:400. And this figure worsens when several members are withdrawn to provide the lucrative security detail services for citizens who can afford to pay. One wonders about why such payments have not resulted to boosts in recruitments for a dedicated security detail corps.

However, with such staffing inadequacy, little wonder that some states started self-help arrangements that have been on for over one and a half decades. Twelve Muslim dominant states of Kano, Zamfara, Sokoto, Kebbi, Niger, Katsina, Kaduna, Bauchi, Yobe, Borno, Gombe and Jigawa formed Hisbah for the enforcement of Sharia law contrary to section 10 of the *1999 Constitution of the Federal Republic of Nigeria As Amended* which precludes the adoption of any religion by any federal or state governments. Some actually call the Hisbah corps religious police. They all operate some elements of vigilantism. In this day and age, they enforce prevention of mixture of gender in public transportation, enforce dress codes, seize and destroy alcoholic drinks etc. There are variations among them. Some like in Kano and Zamfara are based on state laws and are funded by the state and some lack legal backing. The Federal government continues to keep quiet on challenging the constitutionality of any portion of Nigeria being under a separate and additional criminal law beyond the penal code.

The Nigerian Constitution knows Sharia law and gives it equality with Customary law, i.e, focus is on the private affairs of individuals. Of course, Hisbah continues to be in operation. They are expected to complement the police by informing when necessary leaving the police with arrests. But they do more in practice.

The inadequacy of policing in Nigeria did not stop with the complementary religious security arrangements in a constitutionally secular country. Plateau State, under Governor Jonah Jang collaborated with the Federal government and assisted by the UN, set up Operation Rainbow as a civil-military complementary arrangement that was aimed at minimizing insecurity in the State.

Even the Federal government itself contracted private companies to form pipeline surveillance security entities to reduce sabotage on the lifeline of Nigeria: petroleum oil and gas transported through pipelines. Although, this arrangement became an avenue for corruption.

So, it is a surprise that the Attorney-General of the Nigerian federation through a spokesperson on January 14, declared Operation Amotekun illegal arguing the exclusive right of the Federal Government to provide security for Nigeria or any part of it.

This development has resulted in a lot of brouhaha. Does this interpreter of the law have the right to publicly make such a pronouncement without a Federal Executive Council meeting that deliberated and reached a decision? Or in another concern, does the Attorney-General have the power to announce the proscription of Operation Amotekun by the Southwest states without obtaining a court order? Obviously, the answer to these questions can only be in the negative.

Is this statement of the Attorney-General not discriminatory? If it is, why the discrimination against a geopolitical zone that tallies with the Yoruba ethnic group[1] by the Attorney-General? Is it that what's good for the goose is not good for the gander? And if the Attorney-General is being discriminatory, is it not a situation for sanctions since discrimination is abhorred by the Constitution of Nigeria? These are fundamental questions that are yearning for answers.

In the interim, however, it is my view, that the Attorney-General is wrong in claiming the backing of a Constitution this government has been trampling on by concentrating leadership of security and financial concerns largely in the Northwest and Northeast geopolitical zones at the expense of the remaining four zones.

As Governor Kayode Fayemi rightly pointed out, section 14 of the Constitution gives the duty to provide security to the Government which terminology the Constitution also defined as Federal, State and Local governments under section 318. And if the federal, state and local governments share responsibility on security, it would be irresponsible for any of the levels of governance to shark such major responsibility to protect life and properties within territories under their respective governance.

Along this line of reasoning, the Attorney-General erred fundamentally in his January 14, 2020 press statement as he confused the defence of the realm with defence within federating states of Nigeria. While external security is constitutionally within the purview of the federal government, security within federating states is shared by the three levels of government as well as the individual who has the fundamental right to self-preservation under common law and the Constitution.

The inherent right to self-defense has been an inalienable right of every human being at the individual level. Russell on crime puts it aptly thus:
> "...a man is justified in resisting by force anyone who manifestly intends and endeavours by violence or surprise to commit a known felony against either his person, habitation or property.

In these cases, he is not obliged to retreat, and may not merely resist the attack where he stands but may indeed pursue his adversary until the danger is ended and if in a conflict between them he happens to kill his attacker such killing is justifiable...''[2]

Every individual has the first responsibility for his own security. So, if one has the first responsibility for ones security, how can any Attorney-General tell anyone that there is a portion of the Constitution that says Nigeria has the exclusive right to ensure security? After all, it is under this individual right of self-defense that Nigerians build fences around houses and constructed security arrangements within that make mansions become, more or less a prison overnight. Then each house, in some cases have security guards or maiguard as they are called. If a federating state wants to join others to further boost all the individual efforts, how can anyone suggest that the federal government has exclusive right on security? No, definitely not so. The fact is that the inherent individual right to self-defense is at the core of a concentric circles of security. The CDA and local government come next and a geopolitical zone defense network is welcomed to further assist before the federal government wakes up from slumber in the outer core.

That the inherent right to self-defense principle is not limited to the individual is well made under international law. Section 51 of the UN Charter gives Member States of the organisation the inherent right of self-defense easily comes to mind. So, the Southwest Governors have a right to collaborate among themselves and work with willing national security apparatuses to ensure security of lives and properties in the territories under their respective control. Those who elected them into office expect no less.

Self-help by states and geopolitical zones in the face of a nonperforming central government is known to law. If people build and maintain roads, if they generate electricity and provide for water

61

security, etc., as the sovereign state recedes, how can a Judge deny the right to defend ones life and property? Such self-help is necessarily anticipatory. It includes the efforts to "be prepared" in the spirit of the Boys Scout's motto.

Operation Amotekun has been launched. That is the status quo. Operation Amotekun should continue to design and operationalize itself in the Southwest of Nigeria within the law. It should ally with similarly interested States of Nigeria in ensuring enhanced security.

By the way, security is more than carrying guns. Human security has been broadened to be a multi-dimensional enterprise. Even in security qua security, there is so much on surveillance, application of modern technologies, sharing of knowledge in general and intelligence gathering that make the AK-47 redundant. Operation Amotekun need not carry arms to be effective in enhancing the sense of security to allow people to once again feel safe to drive on our unmaintained so-called highways.

The Attorney-General of the federation is weak on moral and legal grounds not to talk of political. Even though this is really a political issue, the Attorney-General should go to court if he likes.

However, since it is the style of the President to keep mum on top, then the Governors should embark on the sensitization of their electors on the options the Southwest faces. This is the time for these Governors to demonstrate that they are leaders.

Executive actions of the type we are faced with are very legal. It is widely used in the United States. In Nigeria, Executive Orders rest on section 5 (1) and (2) of the 1999 Constitution as amended. Section 315 (2) also grants the President or Governor, the power to amend any extant law in order to bring that law in conformity with the Constitution. Executive Orders, have also been decided in Nigeria by the Supreme Court as legal instruments.[3]

Furthermore, nothing in the 1999 Constitution of Nigeria as amended prevents any number of states from entering into collaborative ventures, including on security. One cannot ignore a number of such collaboration like DAWN initiative; the New Nigeria Development Company and on security, the CJTF that brings Borno and Yobe together is a good example.

Nonetheless, one cannot but support additional debates in the Assemblies of the 6 Southwest states on the basis of a model law that can guide the synergy being aimed at under Operation Amotekun. A robust framework that is thought through during the process of debate of the model law that would empower the geopolitical zone collaboration of the respective states would be an added value.

Finally, fundamental political issues are tied to the nature of the security arrangements for Nigeria. These political issues, for long term peace must be discussed and agreed. These would include restructuring that many in the South of Nigeria are clamouring for. It should even go beyond that to address how the constitution will address the poverty character of Nigeria and provide solutions for the underlying causes of insecurity like poverty, unemployment, environmental degradation and desertification as well as effective reduction of corruption. To reduce corruption, the efforts must go beyond punitive sanctions and follow a holistic[4] approach. Meanwhile, arrangements like Amotekun must be embraced as necessary measures.

---

[1]Nigerian geopolitical zones harbor different ethnic groups that are known as original owners of portions of land in spite of limited conflicts. Though changing, emphasis is on origin as opposed to residence as is the case in some other jurisdictions.
[2]Russell W.O (1958) Russell on Crime Stevens & Son Ltd 11th Edition, Vol. 1, p. 491
[3]https://www.barristerng.com/executive-order-no-6-legality-and-constitutionality-by-eloho-yekovie-esq/
[4]Babafemi A. Badejo, "Persistence of Corruption in Nigeria: Towards a Holistic Focus", in Sunday Bobai Agang et. al., A Multidimensional Perspective on Corruption in Africa, (Newcastle upon Tyne: Cambridge Scholars Publishing, 2019), pp. 138-157.

Index

Printed in the United States
By Bookmasters